Rust for Beginners

Herbert M Sauro
Seattle, WA

Ambrosius Publishing

University Disclaimer: Any views, opinions, data, documentation and other information presented in this book are solely those of the author and do not represent those of the University of Washington.

Contents

Preface

This is yet another book on Rust. Surely there are enough books on the market? Plus we have the great 'The Rust Programming Language' at the Rust website itself, and many other websites, videos, and tutorials online.

That may indeed be so, but this book was written out of curiosity, by someone whose never seen Rust before but has, over the years, programmed in a variety of compiled and scripting languages. This book therefore represents a perspective from a beginner. It may not be perfect, it may even get a few things wrong, and it most certainly doesn't cover everything. But it's sufficient to break the ice on the mysteries of Rust and to get someone started. It's not a replacements for the many resources available but a supplement, and one specifically for beginners.

If readers have any comments I'd like to hear about them, corrections to code, terminology or concepts. Goto this website for a contact link:

https://sites.google.com/view/rustforbeginners

This edition was written using Rust compiler version:

`1.87.0 (17067e9ac 2025-05-09)`

I would like to thank my wife, Holly, for her encouragement, support, and patience. Any errors are of course my responsibility.

Herbert M Sauro
Seattle
June, 2025

1

What is Rust

1.1 What is Rust?

Rust is a new programming language that focuses on speed, memory safety, and running tasks in parallel (concurrent programming). It was created by Mozilla and is now developed by a large open-source community.

Rust can be used for systems programming, game development, web assembly applications, and anywhere performance and safety are critical. There is growing interest in using Rust both by hobbyists and by companies. For example, Microsoft just released (May 2025) a new command line editor, `edit`, that is written in Rust. Rust can also be used to build WebAssembly based apps, which allows code to run inside your browser.

1.2 Who is this Book for?

This book is intended for beginners who've had some experience with other programming languages and need a basic introduction to Rust. It is not a comprehensive discussion of Rust and there are lots of nooks and crannies in Rust that are not covered. It is hoped that the information in this book will be enough to get you started in Rust. Once past this book you can advance to other sources of information. I wrote this book because I was curious about Rust. I wanted to know more, so rather than keep what I learned to myself I decided to write a short book on the topic.

1.3 Core Concepts

Here are some of the core concepts of Rust:

Memory Safety Without Garbage Collection: Unlike Python which handles memory automatically, Rust gives you some control over memory without requiring excessive manual management which reduces many common memory errors.

Ownership System: Rust's most distinctive feature is its ownership model, which ensures memory safety at compile time. Each value has an "owner", and when the owner goes out of scope, the value is automatically freed.

Strong Static Typing: Like many compiled languages variables must have their types known at compile time.

Zero-Cost Abstractions: One of the frequent claims is that Rust provides high-level features that compile to efficient low-level code.

Traits: One of the more interesting aspects of Rust is the introduction of traits. These can be used to define an API blueprint which can be implemented by one or more data types. We'll briefly mention these at the end of the book.

1.4 Why Learn Rust?

If you're up for a challenge and want to try out a language that is distinctly different from most other production languages then Rust is worth looking at. If you're coming from Python, Table 1.1 briefly summarizes their differences.

Feature	Python	Rust
Interpreted/Compiled	Interpreted	Compiled to machine code
Memory Management	Garbage collector	Ownership system
Speed	Slower	Much faster
Syntax	Very simple	More strict and complex
Use Cases	Scripts, data science, web apps	Systems software, CLI tools, performance-critical apps

Table 1.1: Comparing Python and Rust

1.5 Isn't Rust Hard to Learn?

Rust can be a difficult language to learn. There are enough differences in syntax and approach to make it harder to learn than other languages. There are three primary reasons for this: The first is that the memory model is quite different and will seem very alien if you've programmed in other languages. The second is that Rust uses significantly more punctuation characters than most programming languages (50 in Rust, compared 32 in C) so that reading the code can be difficult for a newcomer. The third reason is that there a lot of new programming concepts that need to be internalized and this takes time.

Rust however does have some interesting innovations. For example, traits which let's one define shared behavior, enabling polymorphism without inheritance. Traits can be used to define a set of methods and behaviors that a type can implement. Rust also has features found in other languages such as Generics and concurrency support. The main aspect of note, however, is the borrow, owner approach to memory management.

This book is not in any way a comprehensive guide to Rust. The book is intended to **break the ice** so that you can subsequently go on to learn some of the more advanced concepts and the fine details of the language. Half the battle with Rust is just getting started; once you are familiar with the basic constructs and syntax you are more prepared to deal with the more advanced and subtle concepts.

The key to learning any programming language is practice by doing.

1.6 Things you Should be Familiar with

There are some things you should be familiar with: these include the idea of variables, functions and types of data, such as integers, floats, etc. If you've done some Python programming that should be sufficient.

1.7 Things we won't Cover

Here are many things that won't covered, these include:

Advanced error handling	Concurrency
Generics	Macros
Building libraries	Attributes
Box type	Calling external code such as C
Advanced use of enums	Function pointers

2

Some Basic Computer Science

2.1 Basic Concepts

Before we start I'd like to go over some basic programming concepts. If you come from C, C++ or other compiled language then you can omit this chapter. The chapter introduces the idea of pointers and references, as well as the heap and stack. If you know what these are already, you can omit the chapter. This chapter is mainly geared either at new programmers or those who come from Python and may not be familiar with certain memory concepts.

2.2 Pointers

As I am sure you are aware, a modern computer typically has a central processing unit coupled with a large amount of memory. This memory is used to store the running program and any data it needs to work with. To make such data human relatable we invariably assign a label to the data that we can use to refer to the data. For example, in Python, we might store the age of a person in a variable we call age and use a line of code such as:

```
age = 24
```

The number 24 is stored somewhere in memory. The location in memory is called the **address**. The variable age stores the address of the location where the 24 is stored. We say that the variable age **points** to the location in memory that holds the value of 24.

We'll define a **pointer** as a type of variable that holds the memory address of another location in memory. In the above example, the pointer also has the label age so that we can refer to it easily.

What's important is that the pointer doesn't hold the value itself, it holds the location where the value lives, Figure 2.1.

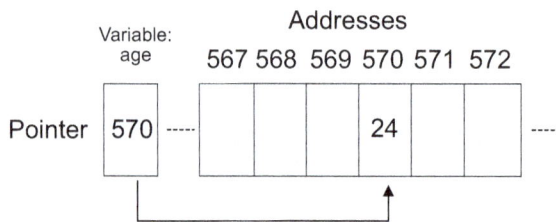

Figure 2.1: A variable age holds a pointer to the actual value, 24, at the memory address 570.

In Python, and some other languages, this can have some odd side-effects. For example, let's say we assign age to another variable called savedAge, like this:

```
age = 24
savedAge = age
```

In Python and most other languages, savedAge points to another location in memory and when the assignment, savedAge = age, is made, the value of 24 is **copied** to the new memory location. This means that if we subsequently change age to another age, the value in savedAge won't change because savedAge points to its own personal copy of 24.

A seemingly odd thing happens when we try the same thing on a more complicated kind of data such as a Python list

Let's look at this example:

```
a = [1, 2, 3]
b = a
b.append(4)
print(a)
[1, 2, 3, 4]
```

Even if you've not used Python before I suspect you can figure out what this code is trying to do. It creates a list of numbers and assigns it to a variable called a. It then assigns a to a new variable b. It appends a new number to the end of b and prints out a. The fact that this code is quite readable is one reason why Python is so popular, but that's another story. There is, however, an odd side-effect. When a is printed out we might have expected [1,2,3], but in fact we got [1,2,3,4]. The designers of Python decided that when assigning lists, that **a copy won't be made**. The reason being that the list could be huge and making a copy of the list could be slow. Instead, **the code copies the pointer** (it a little bit more subtle than that but the idea is similar). As a result a and b hold the same pointer and therefore point to the same data, [1,2,3]. If we mess with b, we are also messing with a. This can come as a bit of a shock to a newcomer but its something you get used to. As an aside, you can make Python actually copy the list as in the following example, and then the side effect disappears.

```
a = [1, 2, 3]
b = copy.deepcopy(a)
b.append(4)
print(a)
[1, 2, 3]
print (b)
[1, 2, 3, 4]
```

Pointers offer a lots of advantages such as:

1. Share large data without copying it
2. Pass values between functions efficiently
3. Create data structures like linked lists and trees
4. Low-level memory manipulation (in operating systems or game engines)

We've been referring to Python variables as storing pointers. However, if that were the case, when we print a variable, such as a, we should see the pointer value not the value it points to. What's happening here is that Python is doing something to help you. It knows a is a pointer but it also knows you probably don't care about the pointer itself but you want the value that the pointer points to. What Python does is called **dereferencing** and often we will say that a is a reference to the value and the value itself is a dereferenced version of a. This kind of language is used a lot in Rust as well as other languages. Although pointers and references are very similar, in Rust references carry additional constraints that are enforced by the compiler. This is to help the programmer write less error prone code.

When we created the list in the previous code, memory had to be allocated to store the list and the elements in the list. What happens if we assigned the variable that points to the list to another piece of data, for example:

```
a = [1, 2, 3]
a = 3
```

In Python, the memory that was used to store the list, isn't just left lying around but it released back to the pool of memory so that the memory can be used again. If this weren't the case its likely we'd eventually run out of memory. Allocating and deallocating memory is called **memory management** and one reason people like Python is that all memory management is invisible to the programmer.

In compiled languages such as C or Rust, you have to handle the memory management yourself. In C, you have to do everything yourself, while Rust gives you a helping hand and tries to protect you from doing bad things. What kinds of bad things? What if you assigned a large list to a variable (Rust does not have lists, it has vectors which are slightly different), then later on you assigned that variable to a simple integer. What if you now forgot that the variable had been reassigned and you now tried to use the list? Your computer program would likely crash since you're trying to access something that is now undefined. Rust tries to protect you from doing things like that by spotting them at **compile time** before you even try to run the program.

2.3   Where is Data Stored

If you read the Rust literature you will frequently find a discussion of where data is stored in memory. This is more so than other languages and is done to help new programmers better understand the mechanics of how Rust works. In a language such as Python, you never worry about where the data is stored so this is an important section if you're coming from Python. In most compiled languages, there are two places where data is stored.

Heap: The first storage area is called the **heap**. This is a general purpose space where we can store lots of different kinds of data. The data **isn't arranged in a particular order**, and the computer will look for any open memory it can find and use it (Figure 2.2). Obviously the computer keeps a track of where everything is. The heap is great for storing very large amount of data that doesn't have a fixed size at runtime. If you want to create a 1000 by 1000 matrix, the heap is the best place for it especially if we don't actually know the size of the matrix until the program starts to run. For example, a program might ask the user what size of matrix they need. More likely the program reads the data from a file in which case it has no idea how much data there is until the data is read in.

Stack: The other place where data is stored is the **stack**. The stack is a **contiguous** stretch of **ordered** memory (Figure 2.2), and the space required for the stack is set up at compile time and hence in general the space is fixed. You can't change the amount of stack space you need once the program is running. Stack space is created whenever a function is called (including the start of the program itself). The size of the stack depends on how many variables a function needs (i.e declares). Because the stack is contiguous (i.e has no gaps), it can only store fixed sized pieces of data. For example, and integer such as 24, may occupy 4 bytes. This is a fixed amount that will never change, hence we can store the value 24 directly on the stack. The other thing that is stored on the stack are pointers which can point to the heap because pointers also have a fixed size (usually 4 to 8 bytes depending on the computer). Fixed sized things like integers, floating point numbers, boolean values, **single** characters and pointers can all be stored on the stack.

One of the convenient things about the stack is that memory management is automatic. When a function is called and it declares an integer variable, say x, the value of x is stored on the stack (because it has a fixed size and the compiler knows how much memory to allocate). When the function exits, the stack is automatically destroyed and along with it any memory it used.

Data that has a variable size can't be stored on the stack. Instead they are stored on the heap. In most compiled languages you have take care of all memory on the heap yourself. In Rust however, it will often manage the heap memory itself by forcing rules at compile time.

The other advantage of the stack is that access to it is slightly faster but I'm not sure how significant that is in the grand scheme of things. Figure 2.2 summarizes the difference between the heap and the stack.

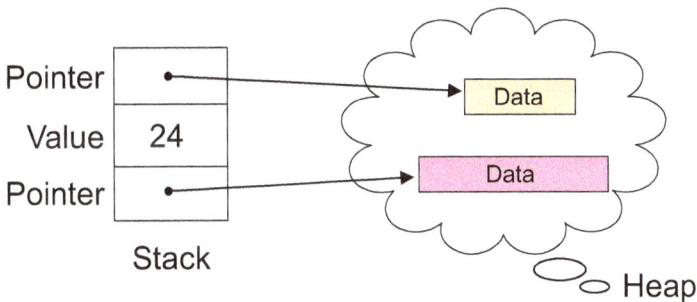

Figure 2.2: Stack: Contiguous ordered memory, limited space; Heap: Unordered, variable size data, large space.

In summary:

1. The stack is for fast, fixed-size data; the heap is for flexible, dynamic data.

2. Rust uses the stack by default, but moves to the heap when needed (e.g., String).

3. Rust's ownership and borrowing rules ensure memory is safe and automatically managed — even on the heap.

Feature	Stack	Heap
Size	Small	Large
Speed	Very fast	Slower (needs allocation)
Ownership	Automatic	Requires explicit handling, but Rust helps out
Clean-up	Automatic at end of scope	Handled by Rust's ownership rules

Table 2.1: Comparison of Stack and Heap Memory in Rust

2.4   Introduction to Ownership and Borrowing

I'd like to give a short introduction to the topic of ownership and borrowing but we will come back to this topic a number of times because its important.

In Rust, ownership and borrowing are fundamental concepts for memory management. Ownership is about who owns a piece of data, and borrowing allows temporary access to a piece of data without transferring ownership. The reason for this unique model is to help prevent memory management errors. There are a couple of useful things to be aware of:

Ownership:

1. Each value in Rust has a **single** owner (i.e variable) at any given time.

2. When ownership is transferred, it is called a **move** and the original owner can **no longer** use the data.

3. When an owner goes out of scope, the value is freed (in Rust this is called a **drop**).

Borrowing:

1. Borrowing uses references, using the symbol, &, to access a value without transferring ownership.

2. Borrows can be mutable or immutable.

3. Multiple immutable references can exist simultaneously.

4. If a borrowed piece of data is mutable (using &mut), then only one mutable reference can exist at a time.

Don't worry if you don't quite understand these concepts, we'll come back to this topic multiple times. I just wanted to give you an initial introduction to the concepts.

3

Setting Up

If you want to forgo the following installation instructions you can. The reason is that there are a couple of very useful online Rust development web sites. For example there is one at `https://play.rust-lang.org/?version=stable&mode=debug&edition=2024`, called the Rust playground. If all you want to do it play around, try some of the Rust syntax and run small programs, this is the best solution to use. There are a couple of these sites available, another one is at `https://www.programiz.com/rust/online-compiler/`.

3.1 Installing Rust

Installing Rust on your personal computer is straightforward. I happen to have a Windows machine so the following installs Rust on Windows. Instructions for Mac and Linux can be found online but they are also straightforward. I will assume some familiarity with the command line terminal. We won't be using a fancy integrated development environment (IDE, e.g, Visual Studio Code) or graphical user interface (GUI) to do this work.

The first thing to do is go to the following web site:

`https://www.rust-lang.org/tools/install`

There you'll find installers for Windows, Linux and the Mac. One wrinkle in the windows install is that if you haven't got Microsoft's Visual Studio installed it will ask you to install it. You won't actually be using Visual Studio but Rust needs the Visual Studio infrastructure to make binary files. Once installed you can forget about Visual Studio.

You can get more information on this topic from:

https://stackoverflow.com/questions/40504552/how-to-install-visual-c-build-tools

Once you have Visual Studio installed, the Rust installation is very fast. It will modify your PATH variable so that when we work from the command line it can find all the files it needs to compile a Rust program.

Once it is complete, start the terminal. To do this go to the start menu and type terminal (that's right, the word terminal). Once you're in the terminal, you will need a place to store all your Rust projects. In my case I created a directory called RustProjects in my Documents folder. But you can put this anywhere you want. You can test your installation by typing:

```
>cargo --version
cargo 1.87.0 (99624be96 2025-05-06)
```

If you're not familiar with the command line here are a couple of commands that you'll find useful:

cd directory	Change directory
mkdir directory	Make a new directory
ls (or dir)	List the contents of the current directory
cd ..	Go up one in the directory structure
notepad filename	Edit a file using notepad

You will need a simple text editor to edit your program code. There are many editors available for this but Windows comes with notepad which is quite acceptable as an editor. Recently Microsoft released a new command line editor call edit. You can get this at the following url if you want to use that (https://github.com/microsoft/edit). Out of interest, this new editor is written in Rust. The advantage of edit is when opened it is part of the terminal itself, where as notepad will be a separate window. Either editor works.

Note, I am using the terminal program, **not** the cmd program on windows. cmd is a legacy application and I don't recommend you use it. If you can't find terminal on your computer, do an online search to get instructions on how to install it.

3.2 Compiling a Rust Program

Small Projects

If you only have a small project with a single file you can use the following approach. This is good for trying small example projects.

Assuming you've created the `RustProjects` directory from the last section, make sure you are in that directory. Inside your `RustProjects` directory, create a project directory for our first example:

```
mkdir myproject
```

Change the directory to your new `myproject` using: `cd myproject`

Inside the project directory create a file called `main.rs`. This is going to store the program code. To create this file you can use notepad or the new microsoft edit editor. It doesn't matter which one you use. If you use notepad, type:

```
notepad main.rs
```

Notice that a Rust source file has the extension `.rs`. Inside notepad, type or copy the following text:

```
fn main() {
    println!("Hello World!");
}
```

Save the file and close notepad (or you can leave it open if you like). To compile our new program type the following:

```
rustc main.rs
```

`rustc` is the Rust compiler. If successful, it will return to the caller and you'll see:

```
>rustc main.rs
>
```

If you see no messages, it means you successfully compiled the program. If you list the files in the directory using `ls`, you'll see a file called `main.exe`. That's your compiled program. To run it, type:

```
>.\main.exe
Hello World!
```

Larger projects

For larger projects, it is highly recommended you use the `cargo` system. Cargo is Rust's build system and package manager. Most people will use this tool to manage their Rust projects because Cargo handles a lot of tasks for you, such as building your code, downloading the libraries your code depends on, and building those libraries.

`cargo` supports a number of functions which are activated using the cargo command. For example `cargo run` will compile and run your project. Notice you don't have to give it the project name, it knows what the name is when you created the project using `new`. Here are a couple of cargo commands that you'll find useful:

cargo new <projectname>	Start a new project (swap <projectname> with your name)
cargo build	Build your project
cargo run	Run your project
cargo test	Test your project
cargo doc	Build documentation for your project
cargo publish	Publish a library to crates.io

Here is an example of using `new` and `run`.

Step 1: To start a new project using `cargo`, change your directory to your `RustProjects` directory, then type the following:

```
> cargo new myproject2
    Creating binary (application) `myproject2` package
note: see more `Cargo.toml` keys and their definitions at
              https://doc.rust-lang.org/cargo/reference/manifest.html
>
```

This will create the directory for the project and all the files it needs.

Step 2: Once you've created your project, `cd` to the project directory: `cd myproject2`. To compile and run your project, use the `run` command:

```
>cargo run
PS D:\Documents\Rust> cargo new myproject2
 Compiling myproject2 v0.1.0 (D:\Documents\Rust\myproject)
  Finished `dev` profile [unoptimized + debuginfo] target(s) in 0.39s
   Running `target\debug\myproject2.exe`
Hello, world!
```

If you list the files in the project folder you'll see quite a few files. The executable file will be in `target/debug`. The name of the executable will by default be `main.rs`.

```
>ls
    Directory: D:\Documents\Rust\myproject2
Mode                 LastWriteTime         Length Name
----                 -------------         ------ ----
d-----         5/20/2025   9:26 AM                src
d-----         5/20/2025   9:26 AM                target
-a----         5/20/2025   9:26 AM              8 .gitignore
-a----         5/20/2025   9:26 AM            153 Cargo.lock
-a----         5/20/2025   9:26 AM             80 Cargo.toml
```

4

Hello World

4.1 Your First Program

Here is the your first program, naturally it's a program to print the message "Hello World".

```
fn main() {
    println!("Hello World!");
}
```

If have a background in a compiled language you'll probably understand this code. The first thing you notice is the keyword `fn`. This stands for **function**. Rust, like most programming languages, has a list of reserved keywords that you cannot use for anything other than as keywords. This means, don't try to use `fn` as the name of a variable, function, etc. It is reserved for Rust's use only. A list of Rust's keywords is given at the end of the chapter.

Following the `fn` keyword is `main`. If you have used C or similar language you'll recognize `main` to mean **this is where the program starts**. Next you'll see two empty round brackets associated with `main`. If you're used to `main` in other languages having arguments, in Rust there aren't any. There is support for retrieving the command line arguments, just not via the main arguments.

Next you'll see an opening curely bracket which starts the block of code that will be run. On the last line you'll see the ending curely bracket. This marks the end of the code block. The code inside the block has a print statement, in this case `println!` which means print something to the screen followed by a new line. If you've come from Python, Rust doesn't uses indent to make blocks of code, but instead uses `{...}`.

This is also where we come across the first instance of punctuation in Rust. In this case the bang or exclamation mark in the print statement. What this says is that print is a special operation called a macro and takes a string as an argument which contains the message Hello World in quotation marks.

Assuming we call the file that contains the source code `main.rs`, we can run this program by calling the following commands:

```
>rustc main.rs
>.\main.exe
Hello World!
```

If you used `cargo new myproject` to create the project, then you'll find that the main file will also be called `main.rs` and will be found in `myproject\src`. `cargo` will also add the hello world code into `main.rs`.

4.2 Compiler Errors

It's inevitable that while writing our code we will make mistakes. When that happens the compiler will tell all about the mistake. The Rust compiler is usually quite good at explaining the problem. Let's make a simple mistake in the hello program. Perhaps we forgot to add the terminating quotation mark to the string, for example:

```rust
fn main() {
    // Missing quotation mark bug
    println!("Hello World!);
}
```

If we try to compile this program the `rustc` compiler will report:

```
error[E0765]: unterminated double quote string
  --> main.rs:2:13
   |
 2 |        println!("Hello World!);
   |   -------------^
 3 | | }
   | |_^
```

```
error: aborting due to 1 previous error
```

```
For more information about this error,
try `rustc --explain E0765`.
```

It even suggests how to get more information by calling:

```
>rustc --explain E0765
A double quote string (`"`) was not terminated.
```

```
Erroneous code example:
```

```
```
let s = "; // error!
```
```

```
To fix this error, add the missing double quote
at the end of the string:
```

```
```
let s = ""; // ok!
```

Understanding errors like this takes practice, so don't expect to immediately figure out problems when the compiler issues an error.

## 4.3 List of Keywords

On the following page you'll see a table of keywords used by Rust. The words in bold are the keywords we'll see used in this book.
```

Keyword	Description
as	perform primitive casting. See official ref for more info
async	return a Future instead of blocking the current thread
await	suspend execution until the result of a Future is ready
break	exit a loop immediately
const	define constant items or constant raw pointers
continue	continue to the next loop iteration
crate	in a module path, refers to the crate root
dyn	dynamic dispatch to a trait object
else	fallback for if and if let control flow constructs
enum	define an enumeration
extern	link an external function or variable
false	Boolean false literal
fn	define a function or the function pointer type
for	loop over items or implement a trait. See official ref for more info
if	branch based on the result of a conditional expression
impl	implement inherent or trait functionality
in	part of for loop syntax
let	bind a variable
loop	loop unconditionally
match	match a value to patterns
mod	define a module
move	make a closure take ownership of all its captures
mut	denote mutability in references, raw pointers, or pattern bindings
pub	denote public visibility in struct fields, impl blocks, or modules
ref	bind by reference
return	return from function
Self	a type alias for the type we are defining or implementing
self	method subject or current module
static	global variable or lifetime lasting the entire program execution
struct	define a structure
super	parent module of the current module
trait	define a trait
true	Boolean true literal
type	define a type alias or associated type
union	define a union; is only a keyword when used in a union declaration
unsafe	denote unsafe code, functions, traits, or implementations
use	bring symbols into scope; see official ref for more info
where	denote clauses that constrain a type
while	loop conditionally based on the result of an expression

Table 4.1: Rust Keywords and their Descriptions. Taken from https://doc.rust-lang.org/book/ with modification.

5

Some Basics

5.1 Comments

Let's start by looking at some basic ideas. The first is the comment. Every programming language lets you add comments to your code. Such comments are ignored
by the compiler. We add them to remind ourselves of what we did and why we did
it. A general recommendation for commenting is comment what your functions do,
the function arguments, return value (if any) and include some text at the top of the
file explaining what it is, author, date, licence etc. Comment other sections of the
code if there is something you think you might not understand at a later time. Avoid
commenting the obvious, although something what is obvious to you, might be a
mystery to another. Use your judgement. Since Rust is relatively new and its programming paradigm is quite novel, commenting is even more important. If you've
come from C or C++, the Rust comments use exactly the same syntax.

```rust
// main is the start of our program
fn main() {
    /*
    This is a multi-line comment
    Its very useful for adding long stretches of text.
    */
    println!("Hello World!"); // You can also add a comment like this
}
```

For single line comments use `// My comment`. For multi-line comments use `/*` ... `*/`. Comments are also a useful debugging aid. If you have a compiler error you can't track down or a strange runtime error you can't identify its source, comment out sections until the error goes away. Now you know where the problem lies.

5.2 Variables: let

You are likely familiar with the idea of variables, they are fundamental to most programming languages. Rust, naturally, also has variables but this will be the first place where we see a difference with most other programming languages. By default, variables are **declared read only**. That's right, the value of a variable, once made, cannot be changed.

Instead, Rust has a key concept, that runs throughout the language, of **mutability** and **immutability**. These words simply mean, something can be changed and something cannot be changed.

In many programming languages, for example C or Python, the idea that something cannot be changed might be alien. Part of the philosophy of Rust is to give the programmer the ability to be more strict on what can and cannot be done. One of those things is to decide if a given value stored in a variable can be changed or not later in the code.

Let's start by creating a variable that can store an integer value. For those coming from Python this idea might come as a surprise. In Python a variable can store any kind of value. In Rust and many other compiled languages, a given variable is created to store a specific kind of data. The reason for this is that the compiler has to reserve space for the data and it needs to know before hand how big that data is. This improves the efficiency of the program when it is run because it doesn't have to figure out much space it needs at runtime.

To create a new variable in Rust we use the `let` keyword. We can make as many variables as we want. For example:

```
// main is the start of our program
fn main() {
    let x = 4;
    let y = 6.7;
    let done = false;
}
```

Rust is will try to guess what kind of variables these are by looking at the right-hand side. For example, the number 4 looks like an integer so it will assume we're trying to create a variable to store an integer.

On the other hand code Rust will assume we're trying to create a variable to store a floating point number in the following:

```
let x = 3.1415;
```

In both cases, the values we store in the variable, x, cannot be changed, that is they are **immutable**. If you were to try to change the values later on, you'll get an error.

To create variables that you want to change later on we have to use another keyword called mut, meaning mutable. We use it like this:

```
let mut x = 3.1415;  // This variable can be changed
```

One thing we've not mentioned are the semicolons. Semicolons are added to the ends of statements. They are not optional. Many languages such as C, Java, Object Pascal use semicolons in this way. They are easy to forget if you're not used to them.

Naming Conventions

Different languages have different naming conventions for variables. Rust uses the so-called snake case convention. This separates words in a variable name with an underscore. For example rocket_velocity. It's similar to Python's convention. I'm not a particular fan of this style (I like camelCase) but that's what Rust programmers are encouraged to use. We'll use this style in this book. Variable names have the usual restrictions, they can't start with a digit but can start with an underscore.

5.3 Print to the Screen

We've already seen a simple example of using the print macro to output a string to the user. There are two print macros to be aware of:

1. print!() This prints the output but does not issue a line feed at the end of the print.

2. println!() This is the same as print except it also issues a line feed.

This means one can use multiple print!() calls and the output will appear on the same line. Here are some examples.

```
print!("This is ");
print!("all on ");
print!("one line.");
```

Output:

```
This is all on one line.
```

```
println!("This is");
println!("on");
println!("multiple lines.");
```

Output:

```
This is
on
multiple lines.
```

The other important aspect about `print` is that it can print other kinds of data in addition to strings. To print out a number we need to use a special syntax:

```
let value = 3.45;
println!("The value is {}", value);
```

Output:

```
The value is 3.45
```

The {} is a placeholder which is replaced by the value of the variable. We can also have more than one place holder, for example:

```
let value = 3.45;
let another_value = 7.8;
println!("The value is {} and the other
                  value is {}", value, another_value);
```

Output:

```
The value is 3.45 and the other value is 7.8
```

If you want, you can also number the place holders so that the values can be printed out in a different order:

```
    let age = 31;
    let name = "Jack";

    // print the variable using println!
    println!("Name = {0}, Age = {1}", name, age);
```

Output:

```
Name = Jack, Age = 31
```

Finally, you can also put the variables names inside the place holder:

```
let age = 31;
let name = "Jack";

// print the variable using println!
println!("Name = {name}, Age = {age}");
```

Output:

```
Name = Jack, Age = 31
```

If you've used other programming languages then you'll be familiar with the new-line character \n. Like other programming languages you can include newline characters in a string:

```
print!("The first line\nThis string is on a second line.");
```

Output:

```
The first line
This string is on a second line.
```

5.4 Declaration and Data Typing

Here is a valid variable declaration in Rust:

```
let foo = 5;
```

There are several things you should notice about this. First, the keyword let. let is used to declare variables in Rust, and must preface every such declaration. Second, if you're accustomed to other statically-typed languages, you've probably noticed that there is no explicit statement of type here; instead, the compiler infers that foo is an integer. Rust's compiler is typically very good at correctly inferring types for variables. However, there are times where it might have difficulty drawing a conclusion, usually when the type of the variable is in some manner ambiguous. We can circumvent this by explicitly telling the compiler what type you want the variable to be, as in:

```
let foo: i32 = 5;
```

i32 means the variable **foo** will be a 32-bit signed integer. We'll cover this notation in detail in the next chapter. Notice the colon, this is similar to how Object Pascal declares variable types. For now, I just wanted you to see what a full declaration would look like.

Just to finish this point, here is a mutable variable also declared as an integer:

```
// Declare a mutable variable to store a 4-byte signed integer
let mut number_of_apples: i32 = 45;
```

Example Small Program

```
fn main() {
    let width = 5.5;
    let height = 8.5;

    let area = width * height;

    // print the variable using println!
    println!("The area of the rectangle is {}", area);
}
```

Output:

```
The area of the rectangle is 46.75
```

6

Basic Data Types

6.1 Basic Data Types

In Rust, data types define the kind of data a variable can hold. Rust has both scalar types (representing single values) and compound types (representing collections of values). The primary scalar types are integers, floating-point numbers, booleans, and characters. There is also the `struct` type which allows one to group data together, we'll see that in a later chapter. **Primitive** compound types include tuples and arrays. By primitive we mean they are built into the language itself. We won't have much to say about tuples but will discuss arrays later on. There are other compound types which are not built into Rust but are defined by external libraries, these include strings, and vectors which we'll look at in future chapters. There are also other interesting types such as a hashmap, but we won't consider these.

We'll first look at the four scalar types.

1. **Integers**: Represent whole numbers. Rust offers signed integers (`i8`,`i16`, `i32`,`i64`,`i128`) and unsigned integers (`u8`,`u16`,`u32`,`u64`,`u128`). Signed integers can represent both positive and negative values, while unsigned integers can only represent non-negative values. The number you see in the encoding, such as the 8 in `i8`, represents the number of bits used to store the integer. Thus 8 represents 8 bits, or a single byte which can store numbers 0 to 255.

2. **Floating-Point Numbers**: These are numbers with decimal points. Rust provides f32 (32-bit) and f64 (64-bit) floating-point types.

3. **Booleans**: Represent truth values (true or false) using the bool type.

4. **Characters**: Represent single Unicode characters using the char type. Rust's char type is up to four bytes in size and can represent a wide range of characters, including emojis.

6.2 Integers

Integers represent whole numbers, such as 2, 5, -7, 999. Integers can be signed, meaning they can represent negative as well as positive numbers, or unsigned where only positive integers are allowed. Table 6.1 summarizes the different kinds of integer. The last row has the architecture specific sizes which depends on the platform. Thus in a 32-bit architecture, the size is 32-bit and on a 64-bit architecture it's 64-bit.

The most common integer to use is probably i32.

Size in Memory	Signed	Unsigned
8-bit	i8	u8
16-bit	i16	u16
32-bit	i32	u32
64-bit	i64	u64
128-bit	i128	u128
Architecture specific	isize	usize

Table 6.1: Table of integer types.

One interesting convenience is that numbers, both integers and floats, can use the underscore character to separate groups of numbers to aid readability, for example;

```
let value = 1_000_000; // This is one million
```

6.3 Floating Point Numbers

Floating point numbers come in two flavours, f32 and f64. These are equivalent to float and double respectively in C, or single and double in Object Pascal. If you do a lot of numerical work then you'll want to work with the higher precision f64 type which represents the IEEE 754 double-precision float. This uses 8 bytes to store a number with approximately 15 significant digits.

To declare a f64 variable use the following syntax (add a mod qualifier if you want the value to be changeable (mutable), see Chapter 5):

```
let value:f64 = 6.58;

// Mutable value
let mod avalue:f64 = 45.67;
```

By default, Rust picks f64 as the type, so that let x = 1.2; will mean that x is of the f64 type.

We haven't introduced the idea of modules yet but I think the following discussion shouldn't be too difficult to understand. There are a variety of constants associated with a floating point number (as well an integers). These can be accessed using the :: symbol. For example, the number of significant digits for f64 can be obtained using:

```
println!("Num digits = {}", f64::DIGITS)
```

Output:

```
Num digits = 15
```

Other constants such as π or e can be obtained from the std::f64::consts module.

```
println!("e = {}", std::f64::consts::E);
```

Output:

```
e = 2.718281828459045
```

One unusual aspect of Rust is how to gain access to the mathematical functions, such as sin, cos etc. Unlike other programming languages which tend to have a math library, Rust attaches these functions to the type. For example, to get the sine of a value we would use:

```
let x:f64 = 5.67;
println!("sin of x = {}", x.sin ());
```

Output:

```
sin of x = 0.8509035245341184
```

The math functions are defined for both f32 and f64. To compute the sine of an integer, such as i32 you need to first convert the integer to a floating point type using a cast (See Chapter 7). However I think the syntax is fairly clear as shown below:

```
let x: i32 = 45;
let sine_value = (x as f64).sin();
println!("sin({}) = {}", x, sine_value);
```

We'll talk more about methods on types in Chapter 17.

6.4   Boolean Values

The `bool` represents a value that can either be true or false. If you cast (Chapter 7) a `bool` into an integer, `true` will be 1 and `false` will be 0.

Those who have used other programming language will be very familiar with the idea of a boolean value. A couple of examples are shown below:

```
let is_valid = true;
let mut check_value = false;
let if_correct:bool = true;
```

`println!()` will print the string true or false for a boolean.

6.5   Characters

The `char` type is for representing **single** characters. The internal representation is based on a 4-byte unicode so that it allows `char` to represents a huge number of characters such as Chinese, Japanese, Korean ideographs and even emoji. Characters are enclosed in **single** quotation marks: for example: `'A'`.

```
let letter : char = 'a';
println!("{}", letter);
```

When dealing with explicit Unicode characters you need to use the \u escape character. For example, the unicode character U+1F601 is the 'Grinning Face with Smiling Eyes' emoji. To specify this character, use the syntax: \u{1F601}.

6.6   Tuples

We won't be covering tuples in this book but here is an example of a declaration of a tuple:

```
let my_tuple = ("Hello", 0, true, -2, 3.14);
```

6.7 Summary of Simple Data Types

Here are some examples:

```rust
fn main() {
    // Integer
    let x: i32 = 10;

    // Floating-point
    let y: f64 = 3.45e-3; // Scientific notation

    // Boolean
    let is_active: bool = true;

    // Character
    let character: char = 'A';

    println!("Integer: {}", x);
    println!("Floating-point: {}", y);
    println!("Boolean: {}", is_active);
    println!("Character: {}", character);
}
```

6.8 Crates, Modules, and Path Separators (::)

Here is a short interlude. Code is compiled into so-called **crates** and one very important crate the comes with Rust is the `std` crate (Rust standard library). This crate contains a lot of useful methods and other functionality. For example, the methods for file i/o are kept in `std`. Many of these are kept in modules which are collections of variables, functions, etc. The path separator, `::`, is used to pinpoint a specific item in a module. To use a particular item in `std` we can use the `use` keyword. For example, there is a module in `std` called `f32`, not to be confused with the type of the same name, though it relates to the same topic. In the module `f32` there is information on the characteristics of the `f32` type. For example,

```rust
use std::f32;

fn main() {
    println!("{}", f32::MAX_EXP);
}
```

Output:

```
128
```

Note: The documentation says in this particular case, the fields in f32 will be deprecated at some point. But its been many years since that was stated.

We'll see more use of the standard library in future chapters.

6.9   Constants

We often require constant values in our software. For example, let's say we need to define the number of minutes in an hour. This is clearly not going to change, so we can make this a constant, using the following syntax:

```
const MINUTES_PER_HOUR: i32 = 60;
```

By convention variables that are constants use upper case. This makes it easy to spot a constant in someone else's code. It's also important to note that constants must have a data type associated with them. Using the line const X = 4; will not compile. This is one of the differences with an immutable variable where the compiler will try to guess what the type is.

Rust has its own defined constants such as a variety of math constants in the standard library. For example, to get Pi, we can use:

```
fn main() {
    let pi = std::f32::consts::PI;
    println!("{}", pi)
}
```

If you want to save yourself from having to constantly type std::f32 every time you refer to a math constant you can also add a use std::f32::consts statement to the start of the file. For example:

```
use std::f32::consts;

fn main() {
    let pi = consts::PI;
    println!("{}", pi)
}
```

7

Operators

7.1 Introduction

An operator is a symbol represented by one of more characters that defines operations on values or variables. For example, + is an operator that performs addition between two values.

Rust programming provides various operators that can be categorized into the following major groups:

- Arithmetic Operators
- Compound Assignment Operators
- Logical Operators
- Comparison Operators

7.2 Arithmetic Operators

Arithmetic operators are used to perform addition, subtraction, multiplication, and division. The following table shows a list of arithmetic operators in Rust.

Operator	Example
+ (Addition)	$a + b$
- (Subtraction)	$a - b$
* (Multiplication)	$a * b$
/ Division)	a/b
% (Remainder)	$a \% b$

```
fn main() {
    let a = 20;
    let b = 2;

    // add two variables using + operator
    let x = a + b;
    println!("{} + {} = {}", a, b, x);

    // subtract two variables using – operator
    let y = a - b;
    println!("{} - {} = {}", a, b, y);

    // multiply two variables using ∗ operator
    let z = a * b;
    println!("{} * {} = {}", a, b, z);
}
```

Power Operator

You might have noticed there is no power operator. For example, you can't type 2^4. The power function is defined as a method on the type, just like the trigonometric functions, e.g on an integer or float. For example, to do the calculation 2^4, where 2 and 4 are integers, you would use x = y.pow (4); where y is defined as an i32 and equals 2. For floating point powers, you need to use the alternative function powf. This is shown below:

```
fn main() {
    let x:f64 = 6.5;
    let y:f64 = 2.3;
    let z = x.powf(y);
    println!("{}", z)
}
```

7.3 Compound Assignment Operators

If you come from C, or Python, the following operators will be familiar to you. They are short-cuts for certain common operations.

For example, a common assignment operator is x += y. This is known as an addition assignment. It first adds y to the value of x and assigns the final result to x. It's equivalent to x = x + y. The table below shows the other assignment operators.

Operator	Example	Equivalent operation
+= (addition assignment)	a += b	a = a + b
-= (subtraction assignment)	a -= b	a = a - b
*= (multiplication assignment)	a *= b	a = a * b
/= (division assignment)	a /= b	a = a / b
%= (remainder assignment)	a %= b	a = a % b

Compound assignments can be optimized for performance by the compiler.

7.4 Comparison Operators

Comparison operators are used to compare two values or variables. For example,

```
3 < 9   // Will yield true
```

Such relations always return a boolean value. 3 < 9, for example, will return true. Table 7.1 shows a list of operators. Notice the == operator. Many languages use the double equals sign as a means to test for equivalence. If you come from a C or Python background you'll know the problems you can get into by using a single = instead of a double ==. You can see examples of comparison operators below.

Operator	Example	Description
> (Greater than)	a > b	true if a is greater than b
< (Less than)	a < b	true if a is less than b
>= (Greater than or equal to)	a >= b	true if a is greater than or equal to b
<= (Less than or equal to)	a <= b	true if a is less than or equal to b
== (Equal to)	a == b	true if a is equal to b
!= (Not equal to)	a != b	true if a is not equal to b

Table 7.1: List of comparison operators.

Operator	Description Example
&& (And)	The operator returns true only if all the expressions specified return true (A > 10 && B > 10) is false
|| (OR)	The operator returns true if at least one of the expressions specified return true (A > 10 || B > 10) is true
! (NOT)	The operator returns the inverse of the expressions result. For E.g.: !(9>5) returns false and !(A > 10) is true

Table 7.2: List of Basic Logical Operators. Results assume A = 5 and B = 12

7.5 Logical Operators

Logical Operators are used to combine two or more conditions and return a Boolean value. Some of these are shown in Table 7.2. These symbols are the same symbols use in languages such as C, Java, etc, although some languages use the more readable and, or, not, symbols. There are also a range of bitwise operators which we won't cover here.

```
fn main() {
    let a = 7;
    let b = 3;

    // use of comparison operators
    let c = a > b;
    let d = a < b;
    let e = a == b;

    println!("{} >= {} is {}", a, b, c);
    println!("{} <= {} is {}", a, b, d);
    println!("{} == {} is {}", a, b, e);
}
```

Here are examples of using the logical operators:

```
fn main() {
    let a = 20;
    let b = 30;

    if (a > 10) && (b > 10) {
        println!("true");
    }
    let c = 0;
```

```
    let d = 30;


    if (c > 10) || (d > 10) {
        println!("true");
    }
    let is_blue = false;

    if !is_blue {
        println!("Is not blue");
    }
}
```

Output:

```
true
true
Is not blue
```

7.6 Type casting

Rust is a statically typed language, meaning all variables must have a known type at compile time. Type casting is used when you need to convert a value from one type to another explicitly.

Rust does not do implicit type casting (also called coercion), like assuming an integer is a float. You must use the as keyword to cast between primitive types. Note you cannot cast between the primitive types and more complex types such as string and vectors.

The following will convert the floating point value 42.9 to an i16. Since i16 is an integer the cast will truncate the decimal part, so y becomes 42.

```
let x: f64 = 42.9;
let y: i16 = x as i16;
```

Here are some common type castings.

Integer to Integer:

```
let x: i32 = 1000;
let y: u16 = x as u16; // Narrower type
```

Integer to Float (You'll need to think about this one):

```
let x: i32 = 300;
let y: u8 = x as u8; // 300 % 256 = 44
println!("{}", y);   // Output: 44
```

Float to Integer:

```
let f: f32 = 3.7;
let i: i32 = f as i32;   // Truncates to 3
```

Char to Integer:

```
let c: char = 'A';
let ascii_code: u8 = c as u8;        // 65 which is ASCII for the letter A
let back_to_char: char = ascii_code as char;
```

You can also cast boolean values to their underling values. When a bool is cast to an integer, true becomes 1 and false becomes 0.

```
let boolean_value: bool = true;
let integer_value: i32 = boolean_value as i32;
println!("{}", integer_value); // Output: 1

let another_boolean: bool = false;
let another_integer: i32 = another_boolean as i32;
println!("{}", another_integer); // Output: 0
```

8

Modules and use

Most programming languages have the ability to create software libraries, that is reusable code. In Rust, such reusable libraries are called **crates**. This chapter will briefly discuss this topic. One of the issues with learning Rust is that the Rust terminology is a little different from other languages.

8.1 Modules and mod

Modules and the use keyword were briefly mentioned before but here we'll go into more detail. This area is potentially confusing to beginners so we will keep it as simple as possible.

In Rust, a module is like a section of code that groups related functions, types, and constants together. A module is a way to organize your code into smaller, reusable parts. It's also a useful mechanism for adding a namespace to a group of items. Of significance is the following point:

A file containing code is also considered a module.

The name of the module, in the case of a file, is the name of the file itself. For example, here is a file called, my_library.rs:

```
pub fn get_rocket_velocity() -> f64 {
    return 100.0;
}
```

The module is therefore called `my_library`. There are a couple of things here that we've not seen before. The first is we're defining a function. I know we've not introduced functions yet but if you've done some programming before the syntax shouldn't be too difficult to understand*.

In brief, a function starts with the keyword `fn`, followed by the name of the function, followed by zero or more arguments with their types specified and an optional return value, also with the type specified.

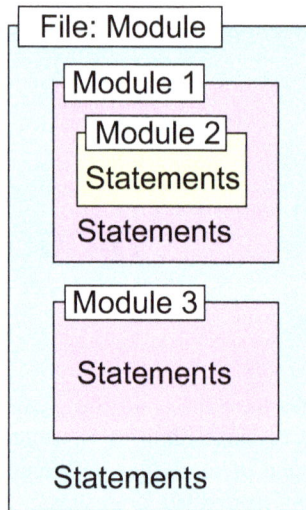

Figure 8.1: Module Hierarchy with a file. The file itself is considered a module.

In the example, the function `get_rocket_velocity`, takes no arguments but returns a double floating point value. I am also using an explicit `return` keyword to make the function return with the value, but more of that in a later chapter.

The other new keyword is pub. This ensures that the function is visible **outside** the file. If you leave this out, the function is only accessible inside the file itself.

To access our new library from another file we need to use the `mod` keyword, short for module. For example, here is my `main.rs` file where I import `my_library`.

```
mod my_library;

fn main() {
  println!("Rocket velocity = {}",my_library::get_rocket_velocity());
}
```

---

*I wouldn't recommend learning Rust unless you have had some experience with another programming language.

Notice how I access the `get_rocket_velocity` function, I use the name of the library followed by `::`, then the function name.

I can also create other modules inside a file. This is useful if you want to separate functions into different groups. To create a new module inside a file use the `mod` keyword followed by the name of the module, then the code. For example, let's create a 'math' module inside `my_library` and call it `math`.

In the example below I've created two functions and a constant inside a module.

```rust
// File: my_library.rs

// Create a math module, make sure the module is public
pub mod math {
    pub const AVOGADRO: f64 = 6.22E23;

    pub fn add(a: i32, b: i32) -> i32 {
        a + b
    }

    fn subtract(a: i32, b: i32) -> i32 {
        a - b
    }
}
```

The `add` function is visible because it uses the `pub` keyword and the other, `subtract`, doesn't. `subtract` is therefore **invisible** to anything outside the module. In this case it's also a fairly pointless function. If you try to compile this code, the Rust compiler will warn you that your're not using `subtract`. The constant is also visible because it uses `pub` keyword. Recall that by convention identifiers for constants are generally in uppercase.

One thing that is easily missed is that the module itself must be made public if we want to access it from outside the file. As a result I've added a `pub` in front of the module as well.

To use this new module we first import it as before using `mod my_library`. We can then call the `add` method using `my_library::math::add`. Noticed how we used `::` to work our way to the method. Modules can be very hierarchical like this.

```rust
mod my_library;

fn main() {
    let sum = my_library::math::add(2, 3);
    println!("2 + 3 = {}", sum);
    println!("Avogadros's number = {}", my_library::math::AVOGADRO)
    // my_library::math::subtract(5, 3);  // Error! subtract is private
```

```
}
```

You don't have to put modules in separate files, you can also add a module to the main file. This is shown below.

```
mod math {
    pub const AVOGADRO: f64 = 6.22E23;

    pub fn add(a: i32, b: i32) -> i32 {
        a + b
    }

    fn subtract(a: i32, b: i32) -> i32 {
        a - b
    }
}

fn main() {
    let sum = math::add(2, 3);
    println!("2 + 3 = {}", sum);
    println!("Avogadros's number = {}", math::AVOGADRO)
    // math::subtract(5, 3);   // Error! subtract is private
}
```

Again, notice how we access the add method, but **also notice** we don't have to use pub on the module because it's in the same file and is automatically visible to other things inside the file. The subtract is still private however, and pointless in this case.

Modules can be very hierarchical as shown in Figure 8.1. Make sure you use the pub keyword if you want inner modules to be visible outside.

8.2   use Keyword

We have seen the keyword use used in some examples already. Your first impression might be that its used to import libraries (crates), **it's not**. What it's used for is to bring items into scope that have **already** been imported.

For example, let's say we were fed up typing my_library::math all the time in order to gain access to the add method in math.rs. What we can do is the following:

```
mod my_library;
use my_library::math::add;
```

```
fn main() {
    let sum = add(2, 3);
    println!("2 + 3 = {}", sum);
}
```

Using this technique we can call the add method directly. If you have a lot of methods in math you can also use the * character to indicate 'everything':

```
mod my_library;
use my_library::math::*;

fn main() {
    let sum = add(2, 3);
    println!("2 + 3 = {}", sum);
}
```

Or if you want to be more specific you can use the following, assuming sub is public:

```
mod my_library;
use my_library::math::{add,sub};

fn main() {
    let sum = add(2, 3);
    println!("2 + 3 = {}", sum);
    let diff = sub (5,3); // Assumes sub is public
    println!("5 - 3 = {}", diff);
}
```

Remember, mod brings in the actual library, but we can use use to simplify access to the contents of the library.

8.3 Built-in Functionality

Rust has a lot of built-in functionality in the form of the standard library, std, and use is used to gain access to this because Rust already knows about its existence so we don't have to 'mod' it in. Things like arrays, char, integers, Vec, String etc are all in the standard library.

9

Decision Making

9.1 The If Statement

In Rust, the `if` conditional statement is used to control the flow of a program by executing code based on whether a condition evaluates to `true` or `false`.

Basic Syntax

```
if condition {
    // code runs if condition is true
} else {
    // code runs if condition is false (optional)
}
```

The condition must yield a boolean value. Unlike some languages (like C or Python), the condition in an `if` statement in Rust must explicitly evaluate to a `bool`. You cannot use integers or other types directly as conditions, for example `if 1 {` is not allowed.

You can use `else if` for multiple branches:

```
if x < 0 {
    println!("Negative");
} else if x == 0 {
```

```
    println!("Zero");
} else {
    println!("Positive");
}
```

if as an expression

if can be used in an expression, meaning if can return a value that can be used in a let statement. All branches must return values of the same type:

```
let number = if condition { 5 } else { 10 };
```

Example

```
let temperature = 30;

if temperature > 25 {
    println!("It's hot!");
} else if temperature < 10 {
    println!("It's cold!");
} else {
    println!("It's moderate.");
}
```

In summary, Rust's if statement is strict about type safety (requiring a bool) and supports expression-style usage.

9.2   Enumerations or enums

Before we can introduce the next topic related to decision making we need to introduce the enumerated type. Many languages support enumerated types so you may be familiar with them already. Rust takes it a bit further.

In its simplest form, an enumerated type, often referred to as an 'enum', is a data type that defines a set of named constants. These constants, typically represent a specific set of values like days of the week or colors. Here is an example of an enumerated type in Rust:

```
enum Colors {
    Red, Blue, Green, Yellow, Orange
}
```

Each of the words is called a **variant**, hence Colors has five variants. Once defined we can assign the 'words' to variables. You can also use them in if statements, for example:

```
#[derive(PartialEq)]
enum Colors {
  Red, Blue, Green, Yellow, Orange
}

let myColor = Colors::Blue

if myColor == Colors::Red {
  println!("The color was red")
} else {
  println!("The color was blue")
}
```

The use of the `if` statement in the above code is a very classical way of using enums in other languages. In Rust you can use the classical way but you also have the option of using `match` which tends to be more favoured as we'll see in the next section. Either will work, what matters is clarity.

You may have noticed one odd thing about the code above. When defining the enum we had to add the line `#[derive(PartialEq)]`. This construct is called an **attribute** and some other languages such as Object Pascal or C# has a similar feature. We won't discuss attributes in this book but the reason we use the PartialEq attribute is that enums can be a lot more complicated than the example shown above and there might be no obvious way to compare them for equality. Rust is intentionally explicit about what operations are available on a type. PartialEq, Clone, Debug, etc., are called traits (Chapter 17) and are opt-in via the derive attribute or by manual implementation. The reason for this is to encourage intentionality. This kind of philosophy can take time to get used and is another reason why it can take a while to master Rust.

enums with values

In Rust, we can also create enums where the enum variants are of different data types such as integers, doubles, strings etc. This is a new feature that other programming languages might not have. Here is an example of such an enum:

```
#[derive(Debug)]
enum MyResult {
      Score(f32),
      Valid(bool),
      State(i32,f32,bool),
}
```

Add the line `#![allow(dead_code)]` to the start of the code if you want to suppress the dead code warnings.

This has three variants, called Score, Valid and State, but in addition, each variant has a value associated with it. The last variant has multiple values associated with it. For C programmes, this is somewhat like a Union, meaning an enum variable of this type can only have one of these variants at any one time. Notice there is a redundant comma on the last variant. This is optional but many Rust programmes include this comma for stylistic reasons. We can set such enums as follows:

```rust
fn main {
    let num = MyResult::Score(6.7);
    let is_valid = MyResult::Valid(false);
    let state = MyResult::State(24,3.14,true);

    println!("num = {:?}", num);
    println!("is_valid = {:?}", is_valid);
    println!("state = {:?}", state);
}
```

Output:

```
num = Score(6.7)
is_valid = Valid(false)
state = State(24, 3.14, true)
```

The special symbol :? in the print statement is use to print out more complex types. A very common place to use enums is when using match which we'll see in the next section. The other very important area that enums and match are used is in error handling. We'll see this in the next chapter.

9.3 Match (Switch Statements)

Most programming languages, except Python (until 3.10), have a means, other than the if statement, to execute code based on the value of a variable or expression. This often uses the switch or case keyword. Rust has a similar ability but it uses the match keyword.

The basic syntax for match is straightforward:

```rust
match value {
    pattern1 => expression1,
    pattern2 => expression2,
    _ => default_expression,
}
```

In the above code, `value` is the item we're matching. Each pattern is checked in order. The _ is the catch-all pattern and is like an 'else'.

Here is an example:

```
let number = 3;

match number {
    1 => println!("One"),
    2 => println!("Two"),
    3 => println!("Three"),
    _ => println!("Something else"),
}
```

Output:

```
Three
```

`match` also lets you match with ranges, for example:

```
let age = 17;

match age {
    0..=12 => println!("Child"),
    13..=19 => println!("Teenager"),
    _ => println!("Adult"),
}
```

`match` is very useful when combined with enums, as shown below:

```
enum Direction {
    Up,
    Down,
    Left,
    Right,
}

let dir = Direction::Left;

match dir {
    Direction::Up => println!("Going up"),
    Direction::Down => println!("Going down"),
    Direction::Left => println!("Going left"),
    Direction::Right => println!("Going right"),
}
```

`match` can also be used to identify enums with specific data values. For example, let's say we define the following enum that has two variants. The first variant can store a byte and the second variant can store two pieces of data, an integer and a character.

```
enum Result {
    Success(u8),
    Failure(i16, char),
}
```

We can use a `match` to check for various combinations of these. In the following example, the underscore means 'anything'. For example, `Failure(25, _)`, will match `Failure` that has an integer value of 25 but any character. The match `Failure(_,_)` lets you match any `Failure` variant.

```
// Here are two different outcomes, comment one out
let outcome = Result::Success(1);
let outcome = Result::Failure(25, 'X');
match outcome {
  Result::Success(0) => print!("Result: 0"),
  Result::Success(1) => print!("Result: 1"),
  Result::Success(_) => print!("Result: Anything success"),
  Result::Failure(25, 'A') => print!("Error: 25 A"),
  Result::Failure(25, _) => print!("Error: 25"),
  Result::Failure(_, 'B') => print!("Error: B"),
  Result::Failure(_, _) => print!("Error: Any failure"),
};
```

These kinds of 'super-enums' are used extensively for error handling which we'll see in the next chapter.

`match` (and enums) are a rich area in Rust but this should be enough to get you started.

match can Return a Value

`match` has one more tick up its sleave. It can return a value, that value being the match it made. This will turn out to be very useful.

```
let coin = Coin::Penny; // Assuming Coin is an enum

let value_in_cents = match coin {
    Coin::Nickel => 5,
    Coin::Dime => 10,
    Coin::Dime => 10,
};
```

10

Loops

10.1 Loops

A loop is a programming structure that repeats a sequence of instructions until a specific condition is satisfied. Rust has three types of loops:

- For loop

- While loop

- Loop

10.2 For Loop

In Rust, the `for` loop is used to iterate over elements in a collection or a range. It automatically handles iteration and avoids common errors like going out of bounds.

The basic syntax for a for loop is:

```
for variable in iterable {
    // code block
}
```

- `variable` takes the value of each item in the `iterable`.

- Common iterables include ranges, arrays, slices, vectors, and iterators.

Example 1: Loop Over a Range

```
for i in 1..5 {
    print!("i = {},", i);
}
```

Output:

```
i = 1,i = 2,i = 3,i = 4,
```

`1..5` is a range that includes 1 through 4 (but **not** 5). If you want to include 5:

```
for i in 1..=5 {
    println!("i = {}", i);
}
```

Example 2: Loop Over an Array

```
let numbers = [10, 20, 30];

for num in numbers {
    println!("Number: {}", num);
}
```

Example 3: Loop with Index Using `.enumerate()`

```
let names = ["Alice", "Bob", "Carol"];

for (index, name) in names.iter().enumerate() {
    println!("{}: {}", index, name);
}
```

Example 4: Loop Over a Vector

```
let mut vec = vec![1, 2, 3];

for i in vec {
    println!{"{}", i);
}

println!("{:?}", vec); // [2, 4, 6]
```

Example 5: Reverse Loop

```
for i in (1..=5).rev() {
    println!("Countdown: {}", i);
}
```

The for loop is often the preferred loop construct in Rust when dealing with known ranges or iterable structures. However, there is more to the for than covered here but for everyday use its a straightforward loop to use. We haven't introduced arrays or vectors yet but I think the syntax is fairly self-explanatory.

10.3 While Loop

The while loop is used to repeatedly execute a block of code as long as a specified condition remains true. It's most useful when the number of iterations isn't known in advance.

The basic syntax for a while loop is:

```
while condition {
    // code to execute while condition is true
}
```

1. The condition must be of type bool.

2. The condition is evaluated **before** each iteration.

3. If the condition is false initially, the loop body won't execute at all.

Example 1: Counting Down

```
let mut count = 5;

while count > 0 {
    println!("Count: {}", count);
    count -= 1;
}
println!("Lift off!");
```

Output:

```
Count: 5
Count: 4
Count: 3
Count: 2
Count: 1
Lift off!
```

Example 2: Reading Until Input is Correct

```
use std::io;

let mut input = String::new();

while input.trim() != "yes" {
    input.clear();
    println!("Type 'yes' to continue:");
    io::stdin().read_line(&mut input).unwrap();
}
```

I know there is a material here we haven't covered but I think its undebatable. This loop keeps asking the user until they type "yes". The unwrap() call is a lazy way to deal with any errors. During experimentation is a useful call to use. If there is no error read_line will grab the text. If there is an error however, the unwrap() will abort the application, a so-called panic response. In production code you'd normally try to detect the error and handle it more gracefully.

Example 3: Infinite Loop with Break Condition

The break keyword can be used to break out of a loop as shown below:

```
let mut n = 0;

while n < 10 {
    if n == 7 {
        println!("Breaking early at {}", n);
        break;
    }
    println!("n = {}", n);
    n += 1;
}
```

Here, the loop exits early when n == 7. You'll find break used in other languages and it operates here in a similar way. Be careful to update the condition variable inside the loop, or you'll create an infinite loop.

10.4 Loop

In Rust, the loop construct creates an **infinite loop** — a block of code that runs repeatedly without checking any condition unless explicitly told to stop using break.

The basic syntax for a loop is:

```
loop {
    // code that runs forever unless you break
}
```

This is Rust's most primitive looping construct. It is often used when you don't know how many times you'll need to loop or you want full manual control over loop exit (using break and continue), or you need to return a value from the loop.

The continue keyword is useful for skipping the current iteration of any loop and moving to the next iteration.

Example 1: Infinite Loop with break

```
let mut count = 0;

loop {
    println!("Count: {}", count);
    count += 1;

    if count == 5 {
        break;
    }
}
```

Output:

```
Count: 0
Count: 1
Count: 2
Count: 3
Count: 4
```

The loop runs until count == 5, then break exits it.

Example 2: Loop Returning a Value

Interestingly loop can return a value and that value can be set in the break statement.

```
let mut counter = 0;

let result = loop {
    counter += 1;

    if counter == 10 {
        break counter * 2;   // returns 20
    }
```

```
};
```

```
println!("The result is {}", result);
```

The break statement can include a value, which is returned as the result of the loop expression.

Example 3: Nested Loops with break **and** continue

Another way to break out is to label a loop so that one can break to a specific loop. This is useful in nested loops. In the example below we have labelled the outer loop.

```
let mut outer = 0;

'outer_loop: loop {
    let mut inner = 0;

    loop {
        println!("outer: {}, inner: {}", outer, inner);
        if inner == 2 {
            break;
        }
        if outer == 1 {
            break 'outer_loop; // the quote is part of the syntax
        }
        inner += 1;
    }

    outer += 1;
}
```

Here, outer_loop is a labeled loop, which allows us to break to the outer loop even when nested.

The loop keyword is ideal when you want maximum control over loop behavior, especially in low-level or performance-critical code.

11

File and User Input

11.1 User Input

A lot of modern software use graphical user interfaces (GUIs), meaning that a user interacts with the software via the mouse. It is possible to write GUI applications using Rust but this is a more advanced topic. The alternative is to write command line applications. However, command line applications need some way to gather input from the user. This is one of the topics of this chapter. We'll first consider reading from the console.

Console Input: To read from the console you will need to use the `read_line` method from `std::io::stdin`. The code below shows an example.

```rust
use std::io::stdin;

fn main() {
    println!("What's your name?");

    let mut input = String::new();
    stdin().read_line(&mut input).expect("Failed to read line");

    println!("Hello, {}!", input.trim());
}
```

The first line uses 'use std::io::stdin' to help reduce some unnecessary text in the code. In the body of the code we first issue a message asking for a name. We then create a new empty string called input, this will eventually hold the input. I know we haven't covered strings yet (Chapter 14) but I think you can figure out that the new call makes a new empty string for us.

We then call read_line. read_line also has an optional expect() call attached to it. read_line could fail and one way to check for this is to use expect. The reason this works is because read_line returns an enum type that represents the possibility of success or failure. The expect call will look at the enum and decide if there was an error or not. This is a common approach to how Rust's handles errors. If you've use exceptions in other languages, you may notice that Rust doesn't support exceptions. Instead, like C, all errors are handled via error codes. But unlike C, errors are handled via the use of enums which can contain multiple values.

You'll also notice that the input variable in the argument of read_line has a strange looking setup: &mut input. What does &mut mean? mut we've seen before, it means mutable. That is we want to allow read_line to update the variable input and change it. However, the string type is one of those special data types that is stored on the heap because at runtime it could have any length. This means the stack entry for input will hold a reference to the string that is on the heap. To give the function access to the reference we indicate this with the & symbol. Collectivity &mut is called a **mutable reference**. The & symbol can also be thought an indicator to tell the compiler that read_line can 'borrow' the string, that is ownership remains with the original variable input but read_line would like temporary access. The &mut syntax is quite general and can be used with other types of data when passing to a function. As part of Rust protection mechanism, &mut also guarantees that input can only be used by read_line for the duration of the borrow.

The expect call checks for an error and will bail out of the application with an error message if there is an error which may not be the nicest thing to do. If you need more control we need to look at the enum that is returned by read_line. This enum has a very specific structure containing two variants: Ok(n) and Err(error). In this case n is the number of characters returned and error is the error message. A common pattern is to use match (See previous chapter) to look for which variant, Ok or Err was returned.

The code below shows how we have more control over any returned error. The big change is the use of match which takes the output from read_line and looks at the enum. The enum has two possible values Ok(n) or Err(error). Recall that the underscore in Ok(_) means any data attached to Ok. If the enum is Ok(_), i.e no error, then it continues and completes the program. Otherwise there must have been an error and so it prints out the error message. The Error variant has the data, error, associated with it which we can use to print out the error message.

One other thing of note, if the read_line is successful, it also does a trim, that's because the input also includes the end of line marker (LF or CRLF), and we can use trim to remove it.

```
use std::io;

fn main() {
    println!("What's your name?");

    let mut input = String::new();

    match io::stdin().read_line(&mut input) {
        Ok(_) => {  // In this example we don't care what Ok is carrying.
            // Remove the trailing newline
            let name = input.trim();
            println!("Hello, {}!", name);
        }
        Err(error) => {
            println!("Error reading input: {}", error);
        }
    }
}
```

This way of handling errors is a very common pattern found in Rust code.

11.2   File Input/Ouput

File input and output (I/O) in Rust is handled through the std::fs and std::io modules. There will be constructs in the following examples that you might not be familiar with. If that is the case, continue reading the other chapters then return to this section.

Table 11.1 lists the basic methods for file input/output.

Task	Module	Key Functions
Read file	std::fs	read_to_string, File::open + Read
Write file	std::fs	write, File::create + Write
Append file	std::fs	OpenOptions + append(true)
Error handling	std::io::Result	Use match for error handling

Table 11.1: File I/O Overview in Rust

Rust uses the standard library's std::fs module to work with files. You can: Read from a file, Write to a file (create or overwrite), and Append to an existing file.

Working with files in Rust usually involves handling errors, since files might not exist or permissions might be denied. Rust uses a Result type to deal with these situations.

Reading from a File: Let's read from a file first. In the following example we read the entire file contents into a `String`. The actual read is straightforward, most of the code is to deal with potential errors and opening the file. For example, when we open the file, the file might not exist and so we need to deal with that potential issue.

Although we haven't introduced strings yet, the line:

```
let mut contents = String::new();
```

will hopefully be self-explanatory. It creates a new empty string object called `contents`. Notice we make the variable mutable. The '`::`' is used to refer to static method that constructs the string.

Once we have opened the file we can use `read_to_string` to read the entire contents of the file into the variable `contents`. Again we check for any errors.

Notice that we don't explicitly close the file, this is handled automatically once the file handle, `file`, goes out of scope. The first statement '`let mut file = ...`' does a lot. It tries to open the file, then uses `match` to check for an error, if there is no error, `match` returns the file handle to variable `file`. If there is an error. It prints the error message then returns. Rust code can be quite dense like this and to a beginner such code can be difficult to read. Study it carefully.

```rust
use std::fs::File;
use std::io::Read;

fn main() {
    let mut file = match File::open("example.txt") {
        Ok(f) => f,
        Err(e) => {
            println!("Error opening file: {}", e);
            return;
        }
    }; // Notice the ; because this is a let statement.

    let mut contents = String::new();

    if let Err(e) = file.read_to_string(&mut contents) {
        println!("Error reading file: {}", e);
        return;
    }

    println!("File contents:\n{}", contents);
}
```

Reading One Line at a Time: Here is another example of reading from a file, but one line at a time.

File::open("example.txt") opens the file for reading. The line:

io::BufReader::new(file)

is used to wrap the file in a buffered reader to improve performance; reader.lines() returns what's called an iterator which will work its way through the lines in the for loop. The println! macro is not necessary but illustrates the lines being read by line number. As with the previous example, it uses match line_result to handle errors on a per-line basis.

```rust
use std::fs::File;
use std::io::{self, BufRead};
use std::path::Path;

fn main() {
    // The path to the file
    let path = "example.txt";

    // Open the file using match and assign to variable file
    let file = match File::open(&path) {
        Ok(f) => f,  // Returns f to the variable file
        Err(e) => {
            println!("Could not open file '{}': {}", path, e);
            return;
        }
    };

    // Wrap the file in a buffered reader
    let reader = io::BufReader::new(file);

    // Iterate over the lines in the file
    for (index, line_result) in reader.lines().enumerate() {
        match line_result {
            Ok(line) => println!("Line {}: {}", index + 1, line),
            Err(e) => println!("Error reading line {}: {}",
                    index + 1, e),
        }
    }
}
```

The above code does require some careful reading to understand.

Write to File: The next task we'll show is how to write to a file. The following routine will open a file then write the contents and close. As before we have to handle any errors that might arise. This code is reasonably readable even to someone who has never seen Rust.

```rust
use std::fs;

fn main() {
    let result = fs::write("output.txt", "Hello, Rust!");

    match result {
      Err(e) => {
          println!("Error writing to file: {}", e);
      }
      Ok(_) => {
          println!("Successfully wrote to output.txt");
      }
    }
}
```

Append to a File: The next example will append to an existing file. Notice the use of OpenOptions as well as writing out the raw bytes to the file using b"..."

The line OpenOptions::new().append(true).open("output.txt") is a bit of a mouth full but it basically says "I want to open a file, and if it already exists, I want to append to it instead of erasing it.". The error enum is coming from the open call.

```rust
use std::fs::OpenOptions;
use std::io::Write;

fn main() {
    let mut file = match OpenOptions::new().append(true)
                    .open("output.txt") {
        Ok(f) => f,
        Err(e) => {
            println!("Couldn't open file for appending: {}", e);
            return;
        }
    };

    if let Err(e) = file.write_all(b"\nAppended line!") {
        println!("Couldn't append to file: {}", e);
    }
}
```

12

Arrays

12.1 Arrays

Like many programming languages, Rust can store collections of data elements. The most basic type is the array. Arrays are a **fixed-size** list of elements of the same type. By default, arrays are immutable. By fixed size we mean that the size (i.e length) of an array is set at compile time. Once an array has a given length, it's length cannot be changed. If you want a collection type that can be changed at runtime, you need to use a vector (next chapter).

Technically, arrays are stored on the stack. This means if you declare an array in a function, the array will automatically disappear when the function exits.

12.2 Declaring Arrays

You can declare an array as shown in the example below:

```rust
let a = [1, 2, 3]; // Allocates an array of three integers (i32)
```

By default, arrays are immutable. If you want to be able to change the contents of an array you need to declare it as mutable:

```
let mut m = [1, 2, 3]; // Creates a mutable array of integers
```

You can also declare an array more explicitly by specifying the type, as in:

```
let m:[f64; 3] = [1.2, 2.4, 3.8]; // Creates an array of f64
```

The notation [f64; 3] represents an array type. The first element f64 is the type and the second element 3 is the length of the array.

There's a shorthand for initializing each element of an array to the same value. In the following example, each element of a will be initialized to 99:

```
// Declare space for 20 elements.
// The type is inferred from the first value, 99, in this case an integer (i32)
// The second value determines the length
let a = [99; 20];
```

If you want to print an array you need to use the so-called debug trait {:?} to print a full array:

```
let colors = ["red", "green", "blue"];
println!("{:?}", colors)
```

Output:

```
["red", "green", "blue"]
```

12.3 Assessing Elements

You can access a particular element of an array using the subscript notation:

```
let names = ["John", "Alan", "Sally"]; // names: [&str; 3]

println!("The second name is: {}", names[1]);
```

You can also set values of the array if it's mutable:

```
let mut values = [2.3, 5.6, 7.8, 8.9];

values[1] = 99.99;
println!("The second value is: {}", values[1]);
```

Like most programming languages, subscripts start indexing at zero, so the first name is names[0] and the second name is names[1]. If you try to use a subscript that is not in the array, you will get an out-of-bounds error at run-time.

Length of a Array

You can get the number of elements in an array a with `a.len()`.

12.4   Looping with Arrays

Looping through an array is very simple. This code will print each number in order:

```
let a = [1, 2, 3];

println!("a has {} elements", a.len());
for value in a {
    println!("{}", value);
}
```

This iteration gives you a **copy** of each element in `value` assuming the compiler knows how to make a copy. For example, the compiler knows how to copy all the primitive types.

There is another way you can iterate through an array by using a range which let's you get access via the index:

```
let a = [1, 2, 3];

println!("a has {} elements", a.len());
for index in 0..a.len() {
    println!("{}", a[index]);
}
```

What about looping through an array of strings? That's a more subtle topic. We will cover strings in Chapter 14. If you need to, you can omit this part until you know more about strings.

If the array is a list of literal strings, such as `let a = ["Hello", "World"]`, the looping variable, `value`, will be a reference, `&str`, to the string. If you want an actual `String` type you can clone it using, `value.to_string()`. If your array is an array of `String` types then you need to iterate over the reference to the array, `&a`, and then you can use `value.clone()` to make a copy.

There are a number of other ways to loop through an array, but these are beyond the scope of this book.

12.5   Arrays Slicing

A slice is a reference into an array. They are useful for allowing efficient access to a portion of an array **without** copying. For example, you might want to reference just one line of a file read into memory. Slices have a length, can be mutable or not, and in many ways behave like arrays. The following example creates a slice of the array a.

```
let a = [0, 1, 2, 3, 4];
let middle = &a[1..4]; // A slice of a: just the elements 1, 2, and 3

for value in middle {
    println!("{}", value); // Prints 1, 2, 3
}
```

The slicing syntax has other variants such as &a[..] for the whole array, &a[..3] from the start to index 2, and &a[2..] from index 2 to the end.

If you want to create a mutable slice, use &mut. Remember however to also add mut to the original variable a. For example:

```
let mut a = [0, 1, 2, 3, 4];
let middle = &mut a[1..4]; // A mutable slice of a: elements 1, 2, and 3
middle[1] = 20;

for value in middle {
    println!("{:?}", value); // Prints 20, 2, 3
}
```

12.6   Assigning Arrays

In the following code one array is assigned to another array:

```
fn main() {
    let a = [10,20,30];
    let mut b = a;
    b[0] = 99;

    println!("Array = {:?}", a);
    println!("Array = {:?}", b);
}
```

Output:

```
Array = [10, 20, 30]
Array = [99, 20, 30]
```

The output shows that in the assignment, b = a, a copy of a is made. This isn't like Python where only the pointer is copied. An array of literal strings aren't copied, only the references. With an array of String types, the right-hand side of the assignment loses ownership and can't be used again. However, the compiler will protect you against this.

12.7 Two Dimensional Arrays

There are various ways to create a 2-dimensional array and by extension any dimenson. Here are three ways you can use. I would probably recommend the second way where the type for the array elements is explicit. Recall that the declarative syntax for an array is [Type; size].

```rust
fn main() {
    // A short bit of syntax to create a 4 by 6 array of doubles
    let mut a = [[0.0; 4]; 6];

    a[0][0] = 2.3;

    // Create a 3x4 array to i32 values, all initialized to 0
    let mut b: [[i32; 4]; 3] = [[0; 4]; 3];

    b[0][0] = 45;

    // Or initialize with specific values
    let mut c = [
        [1.3, 2.1, 3.3, 4.5],
        [5.2, 6.3, 7.4, 8.5],
        [9.1, 10.6, 11.3, 12.0],
    ];

    c[0][0] = 2.3;

    println!("Array = {:?}", a);
    println!("Array = {:?}", b);
    println!("Array = {:?}", c);
}
```

The following shows how to iterate through a 2D array called data. Note the use of len() to get the length. For the inner loops we use data[i].len() to get the number of columns in the array.

```rust
fn main() {
    let mut data = [[0u32; 4]; 4]; // Yes, it's 0u32
    data[0][0] = 23;

    for i in 0..data.len() {
        for j in 0..data[i].len() {
            print!("{}, ", data[i][j]);
        }
        println!();
    }
}
```

Notice the 0u32 on the second line. This is an alternative notation for specifying the type of a value. It can even be used when declaring a new variable such as:

```rust
fn main() {
    let a = 46i32; // Declare i32 variable with value 46
    println!("{}", a);

    let b = 3.14f64;
    println!("{}", b);
}
```

Make sure there is no space between the value and the type. For example, 0 i32 is not legal.

13

Vectors

13.1 Vectors

A vector is another structure for storing lists of data elements. However unlike arrays we saw in the last chapter, vectors can be sized at runtime, and can change length as the program runs. Like arrays, a given vector will only store a single type at a time. That is all integers, all doubles etc. There is a way around this using enums but that's another topic. Unlike arrays that are allocated on the stack, a vector is stored in the heap (See Chapter 2).

Vectors can be created using the vec! macro. For example:

```
let v = vec![1, 2, 3]; // Rust infers that the vector will use i32 elements
```

Notice we use square brackets [] with vec! but Rust will also allow you to use round brackets. As with other data types, vectors can be mutable or immutable. Here is a mutable vector:

```
let mut nums = vec![1, 2, 3];
```

A vector has the type Vec<type>, for example, Vec<i32>. You can initialize a vector with a give type and initial values using the following syntax:

```
let v = vec![0.0; 5];
```

This creates a vector of five elements with the type f64. The first element has to be a value, it can't be a type. We will use this form to create two-dimensional vectors in a later section. Here are some more examples:

```
let u = vec![3.14f32; 6] // initialize and specify the type explicitly
// You cannot do this:
let b = vec![truebool, 10] // This will generate a compiler error
// Instead do this:
let b = vec![true, 10]
```

Like arrays, a given vector can only contain one type. This is different compared to say Python lists which can contain a mix of types. To get the length of a vector you can use len(), for example:

```
println!("Number Of Houses: {}", town.len());
```

Accessing individual elements is similar to arrays, you index using a subscript, for example:

```
let colors = vec!["blue", "red", "green"];
println!("The second element is: {}", colors[1]);
```

As with arrays, indexing starts at zero. **The key property** of vectors is you can add new elements to a vector using the push method. For example:

```
let mut colors = vec!["blue", "red", "green"];
colors.push ("orange")
println!("The colors are: {:?}", colors);
```

You can also remove elements from a vector by using the remove method:

```
let mut even_numbers = vec![2, 4, 6, 8, 10];

println!("original vector = {:?}", even_numbers);

// remove value from the vector at index 2
even_numbers.remove(2); // also returns the element if you want it.

println!("changed vector = {:?}", even_numbers);
```

If you just want to remove the last element you can use the pop() method:

```
let mut even_numbers = vec![2, 4, 6, 8, 10];
// remove the last vale in the vector
// Also returns the element unless it's empty which is an error.
even_numbers.pop();

println!("changed vector = {:?}", even_numbers);
```

Empty Vectors

If you want to create an empty vector that will hold a specific type you can use the following code:

```
// Creating an empty vector
let mut v: Vec<i32> = Vec::new();
v.push (10); v.push (20);
```

This will create an empty vector for storing integer values. A new vector must be declared with a specified type.

If you want to create a presized vector for efficiency reasons, you can use the method with_capacity:

```
let mut v: Vec<f64> = Vec::with_capacity(10);
v.push (3.14);
println!("{:?}", v)
```

Looping Through a Vector

The easiest way to loop though a vector is also probably the most obvious:

```
let v = vec![1,2,3,4,5];
for value in v {
    println!("{}", value);
}
```

Here is another example:

```
let colors = vec!["blue", "red", "green"];

let mut index = 0;

// loop through a vector to print its index and value
for color in colors {
    println!("Index: {} -- Value: {}", index, color);
    index = index + 1;
}
```

13.2   2D Vectors

There are various ways to create 2D vectors but we can create one using the `vec!` macro by nesting `vec!` calls. Notice we use the `[value/type;size]` notation which can be nested. For example, `[0f32; 6]`.

```
// Create a 16 by 16 vector grid
// Element type will be single precision float
// If we don't include the type, the compiler will try to infer it
let mut grid = vec![vec![0f32; 16]; 16];
grid[0][0] = 45.0;  // Must use decimal point here
println!("{:?}", grid)
```

We can also be more explicit about the type stored in the vectors as shown in the following example where we make a matrix. Note that we use `0.0` in the `vec!` macro call if we want to store floating point values. Also observe that the matrix dimension is 3 by 4 but the order of declaration is 4 by 3 because its row by column.

```
// Create a 3x4 matrix filled with zeros
// Compiler infers f64 for the type
let mut matrix = vec![vec![0.0; 4]; 3];

matrix[0][0] = 42.4;
println!("{:?}", matrix);
```

You can also create 2D vectors manually by first creating an empty vector then add rows to it as required. This is a common approach to building arrays in C.

```
let mut matrix: Vec<Vec<f64>> = Vec::new();
for i in 0..3 {
    let mut row = Vec::new();
    for j in 0..4 {
        // Add some values to the matrix
        row.push((i as f64) * (j as f64));
    }
    matrix.push(row); // Add the row
}
matrix[2][3] = 42.7;
println!("{:?}", matrix);
```

It is possible to create a large one dimensional vector and use index calculations to mimic a two dimensional structure. Some argue it's faster for access due to a simpler memory layout. The method relies on the formula `[x + y * width]` where x and y are the coordinates for an element and width is the width of a single row.

14

Strings

14.1 Introduction

A string is a sequence of characters, more specifically a string of unicode characters. Before 1991, the characters in a string were the usual culprits, lower case and upper case letters, the digits, some punctuation and a few other bits and bobs. These were the ASCII characters that are stored in one byte. As computing spread out to cultures that had different written languages, the ASCII set wasn't sufficient to represent the many more characters that actually exist in the real world as well as the modern trend for inventing new characters such as emojis. As a result, Unicode was developed which reserved a lot more space for many more characters. If you're interested in more background, the Wikipedia page on Unicode is a good place to visit.

All the characters in the standard ASCII character set can be stored using a single byte, namely 256 characters. For Unicode we need more bytes. A common Unicode standard is called UTF-8 which can use up to four bytes to store a character. Rust strings are stored using UTF-8.

String handling in Rust is surprisingly complicated compared to other languages. One reason is that there are seven different string types. The other reason is related to how Rust handles memory. Two of the seven types, however, are more commonly used than any other, they are: `String` and `&str` which we will look at in this chapter.

14.2   String Literals

When you use something like:

```
let s = "Hello"
```

you are creating what's called a **string literal**. Such strings are hardcoded into the application. The variable s is actually a pointer (or in Rust parlance, a reference because it also contains the length of the string) to the string somewhere in the application executable itself. String literals are related to the &str type. In fact you can declare a literal string as a &str type explicitly:

```
let s: &str = "Hello"
```

Since string literals are burned into the application, they can never been changed and technically they are called static &str. In every case, a &str type is **always immutable**. A &str is a read-only view on to another string, usually strings of type String. This means &str are borrowed and not owned. They are, for example, useful for efficiently passing strings to functions. We'll come back to &str again but it's a reference that includes a pointer to the string characters as well as the length of the string.

14.3   String

String is a growable string and the kind of string we normally associate with strings in other languages. Unlike a literal string such as let s = "Hello"; which is fixed, String is a dynamic type, meaning we can change it (assuming we make it mutable of course). In some sense String is like a Python string. In contrast to &str, a String is owned and potentially mutable. To declare a mutable String you can use the following code:

```
fn main() {
    let mut aString = String::from("Hello World");
}
```

This shows you one of the ways to create a String, from what effectively is a &str type. Another way is to use the to_string method on a literal string, for example:

```
fn main() {
    let mut aString = "Hello World".to_string();
}
```

Internally, the String type is a struct (see Chapter 15) that is stored on the stack.

Within that struct there is a pointer to a memory block in the heap that stores the actual string. In addition, the struct also has the current length of the string and how much capacity is allocated for growth. The later is for efficiency reasons to limit the number of times new memory has to be allocated if the string grows.

There are other ways to create a `String` but these will do for now. You can get the length of a `String` using `len()` as in:

```
fn main() {
    let mut aString = String::from("Hello World");

    println!("{}", aString.len())
}
```

14.4 Growing the String Type

You can grow a `String` type by using the oddly named `push_str` method. The phrase push may come from the C++ standard library where the phrase `push` is used a lot. Append might have been a more readable name to use. In addition to `push_str` there is also push which is used to add a **single character** to a `String`. Here is an example of adding a single character:

```
fn main() {
    let mut aString = String::from("Hello World");

    aString.push ('X');
    println!("{}", aString)
}
```

Notice that `push` does not return anything but changes the string in situ. The next example shows the use of `push_str`:

```
fn main() {
    let mut aString = String::from("Hello ");

    aString.push_str ("World");
    println!("{}", aString)
}
```

The type of string passed to `push_str` is a `&str` type. This can be a string literal or a **string slice**. `&str` is a borrowed string, meaning it's a view into an existing string's data, but it **doesn't** own that data itself.

In the following example, we create a `String`, then create a literal string and append it to the end of the `String` type. The point here is that `push_str` only takes `&str`

types as an argument, you can't pass a `String` to `push_str`.

```rust
fn main() {
    let mut first_string = String::from("Hello ");
    let second_string: &str = "World";

    first_string.push_str(second_string);
    println!("{first_string}");
}
```

Here is a combination of all the methods being used and shows how we can use `String::from` as a reference argument in `push_str`.

If you use the syntax `&String`, this is coerced to a `&str` in the `push_str` call.

```rust
fn main() {
    let mut x = String::from("Hello World");
    x.push('!');
    x.push_str("abc");
    x.push_str (&String::from ("xyz"));

    println!("{}", x)
}
```

14.5 Concatenation

Concatenation of string is a common operation but is surprisingly non-trivial in Rust. Many users have strong opinions on what to use for concatenation. Here are three approaches. The most obvious is just use a series of `push_str` calls which is shown below:

```rust
fn main() {
    let s1 = "The ";
    let s2 = "quick ";
    let s3 = "brown ";
    let s4 = "fox.";

    let mut result = String::new();
    result.push_str(s1);
    result.push_str(s2);
    result.push_str(s3);
    result.push_str(s4);

    println!("{}", result); // Output: The quick brown fox.
}
```

We use `String:new()` to create an initial empty string, though it doesn't have to be empty. If you want to concatenate two `String` types this way you can dereference the second string that can be coerced to `&str`, as in the following example:

```
fn main() {
    let mut s1 = String::from ("Hello");
    let s2 = String::from ("World");

    s1.push_str (&s2);
    println!("{}", s1);
}
```

The second approach is to use the plus operator, '+'. You have to be careful however. Let's first show an example that does this:

```
fn main() {
    let mut result = String::from("A small string");

    let mut newstring = result + "A larger string";
    println!("{}", newstring)
}
```

This works because `"A larger string"` is a literal string which is of type `&str`. The add operator **expects** a `&str` to be on the **right-hand side** of the '+'.

The addition also looks quite harmless but it's not. What is not apparent is that ownership (see Chapter 17) of `result` has been transferred to `newstring`. If you try to use `result` again, for example print it out, you'll get a compiler error. When concatenating strings using '+', the right-hand term must be a `&str` and the left-hand of '+' must be a `String` type. In the process you will lose access to the left-hand string to the left of the plus symbol because ownership gets transferred.

You can, however, include as many `&str` terms as you like with a plus between each of them. Here is an example:

```
let another_string = "Another";
let yet_another_string = "yetAnother";
let result = String::from("A small string") +
                &another_string + &yet_another_string;
println!("{}", result)
```

If you don't want to lose access to the left-hand string, you can instead use `format!`. A lot of Rust developers seem to use this approach. Here is an example that uses both literal and `String` types:

```
fn main() {
```

```
    let s1 = "Hello";
    let s2 = "World";

    let result = format!("{} middlebit {}", s1, s2);
    println!("{}", result); // Output: "Hello middlebit World"

    let s3 = String::from ("Goodbye");
    let s4 = String::from ("World");

    let result = format!("{} middlebit {}", s3, s4);
    println!("{}", result); // Output: "Goodbye middlebit World"
}
```

14.6   Strings to Numbers

One common operation you might like to do is convert a number into a string. A number such as an integer has a method called `to_string`. You can use this to convert a number to a `String` type, for example:

```
fn main() {
  let x = 5;
  let astr = x.to_string();

  println!("{}", astr)
}
```

This will work for floats as well. To go the other way and convert a `String` type to a number you can use `parse()`. For example:

```
fn main() {
  let x = String::from ("3.4");
  let y: f32 = x.parse().unwrap();

  println!("{}", y)
}
```

The `unwrap` in the above code is there because `parse()` doesn't return a pure number but an `enum` that contains the number and an error condition. The `unwrap()` is used to get the number (assuming there was no error).

There is a lot more to strings, but what we've covered above should be enough to get you started. We'll talk more about strings when we discussion functions.

15

Structs

15.1 Structs

A struct is a means to create a more complex data type by grouping things together. For example, you might need to group together the name, height and age. You could have separate variables for these but its more useful to collect them together into a struct. Once defined this way you can create variables of this type. Here is an example of a struct called `Person`:

```
struct Person {
    name: String,
    height: f32,
    age: i32
}
```

A struct contains fields, that represent the pattern of data inside the struct. Notice we don't use `let`, as in `let name:  String`. This is because we're not actually creating anything, we're just defining a new kind of data type.

Once defined we can declare a variable of this type:

```
let aperson = Person {
    name: String::from("John Smith"),
    height: 164.0,
```

```
    age: 24
};
```

Notice that when we declare the variable we also initialize the fields to their initial values. Once declared we can access the fields in the struct using a period syntax. For example:

```
let theirAge = aperson.age;
println!("The person's age = {}", theirAge);
```

If we want to modify the values in a struct we need to make the variable mutable. Here is an example that defines a point and sets the values in a point variable:

```
fn main() {
    // define a Point struct
    struct Point {
        x: i32,
        y: i32,
    }

    // Create a mutable structure variable
    let mut point = Point { x: 0, y: 0 };

    println!("Before change:");
    println!("Point x = {}", point.x);
    println!("Point y = {}", point.y);

    // change the value of x field in mutable point struct
    point.x = 5; point.y = 12;

    println!();
    println!("After change:");
    println!("Point x = {}", point.x);
    println!("Point y = {}", point.y);
}
```

Notice we use the period syntax, . to access a particular field.

16

Functions

16.1 Functions

Functions are extremely useful in software because they promote reusability, make code more organized and readable, and improve maintainability. Almost all programming languages support the creation of functions.

In Rust, functions are defined using the `fn` keyword, followed by the function name and a set of parentheses.

Functions can accept parameters, which are variables passed into the function. Functions can also return a value, which is specified after an arrow -> in the function signature. Functions are probably one of the more difficult aspects of Rust to fully understand which is why I've left it to the end. The complication comes from the various ways in which arguments can be passed to functions as well differences between passing primitive and non-primitive types.

Here is an example of a simple function that takes no arguments and doesn't return a value:

```
fn print_message () {
    printn!("This is a message")
}

print_message();
```

16.2   Returning Values

Before we consider how to pass values to a function, let's consider returning values first, as this is much simpler.

To return a value from a function we add an arrow -> in the function signature followed by the type we wish to return. This is similar to Object Pascal where a colon is used instead of an arrow. Here is an example that returns an integer:

```
fn add (x: i32, y: i32) -> i32 {
    return x + y
}

sum = add(16, 78);
```

Notice that we used the keyword `return` to tell the function to return to the caller. There is another way to return a value which is to just use the expression without the return keyword. For example,

```
fn add (x: i32, y: i32) -> i32 {
    x + y
}

sum = add(16, 78);
```

Personally, I find the use of the `return` keyword more readable though there are Rust developers who will recommend otherwise. However, since source code is read far more often than it is written (especially by people other than the author), clear readability is important. Another reason to use `return` is that a `return` will make the function exit at that point. This can make returns buried in the code easier to see.

16.3   Passing Arguments

In most programming languages, values can be passed to a function in one of two ways, called **pass by value** and **pass by reference**. In Rust there is a third way, the **mutable reference**.

Let's summarize what these approaches are:

Passed by Value: This means a copy of the data is made as it is passed into the function. As a result, any changes in the value inside the function aren't reflected in changes outside the function.

Passed by Reference: This means a reference (a pointer) to the data is passed into the function. In other programming languages this allows a function to change the data inside the function and at the same time change its value outside the function.

In Rust however, this mechanism is different. Not only can't the value be changed outside the function, but it can't be changed inside the function. This may appear completely pointless, but passing by reference is still useful because it avoids making a copy. For example, you may want to pass a very long string to a function, but don't want a copy made. In Rust terminology, we say that the function has borrowed the string and will give it back once it returns to the caller..

Mutable Reference: In Rust when data is passed by reference it can't be changed, so Rust has an additional mutable version, called a **mutable reference**. This allows the data to be changed in the function as well as at the same time outside the function.

The details will become clearer once we look at some real examples. Since we've been using the borrow and ownership terminology, let's quickly review the idea of ownership and borrowing in Rust.

In Rust, ownership and borrowing are fundamental concepts for memory management. Ownership is about who owns a piece of data, and borrowing allows temporary access to a piece of data without transferring ownership. The reason for this unique model is to help prevent memory management errors. There are a couple of useful things to be aware of:

Ownership:

1. Each value in Rust has a **single owner** at any given time.

2. When ownership is transferred, it is called a **move** and the original owner can no longer use the data until ownership is returned.

3. When an owner goes out of scope, the value is freed (in Rust this is called a **drop**).

Borrowing:

1. Borrowing uses references, via the symbol, &, to access a value without transferring ownership.

2. Borrows can be mutable or immutable.

3. Multiple immutable references can exist simultaneously.

4. If a borrowed piece of data is mutable (using &mut), then only one mutable reference can exist at a time.

With that summary in mind, let's first consider the simpler case of passing primitive types to a function. If you recall, primitive types are the integers, floats, boolean and character values.

Passing Primitive Types by Value

In Rust, primitive types like, i32, are, by default, **passed by value**, that is their value is **copied**. This means that changes made inside a function won't affect the original value outside. Here is a function that includes an integer argument in the call and the corresponding call code:

```rust
fn print_value (value: i32) {
    println!("The value is: {}", value);
}

fn main() {
    let x = 32;
    print_value(x);
    println!("{}", x)
}
```

Note that the value of x is still available after the call returns. This is because a copy of x was made for the function. x essentially retained ownership of the value 32, while value in the function got to own its own personal copy. Here is another example with two arguments in the call:

```rust
fn print_sum (x: i32, y: i32) {
    println!("The sum is: {}", x + y);
}

print_sum(16, 78);
```

One thing you can't do in the above code is change the value inside the function. To change the value of a primitive type in the function, you have to declare the argument as mutable. The following example illustrates this idea. Note that the mut is **in front** of the variable name.

```rust
// Pass by value but mutable inside the function
fn change(mut x: i32) {
    x += 1;
    println!("Inside: {}", x);
}

fn main() {
    let n = 5;
    println!("Outside: {}", n);
    change(n);
    println!("Outside: {}", n);
}
```

Output:

```
Outside: 5
Inside: 6
Outside: 5
```

Notice that the value outside the function is still unchanged! In summary, primitives can be passed by value with the option of being mutable inside the function.

Passing Primitive Types by Reference

By reference, we mean that the variable coming into the function is not a copy but the same one that is outside the function.

There are two ways to pass a primitive type by reference. In each case we use the & symbol to indicate a reference. For example, a function argument can be written as a: &i32. This syntax gives us an immutable reference to the argument. We can also use the **mutable reference** notation which would be a: &mut i32. This means the value in the function can be changed.

There is one important wrinkle which for a C programme won't be strange but to a Python programmer will be. What's coming through in the function call when we use a reference is a pointer to the location in memory where the value is stored. To actually get at the value itself, we have to **dereference** the pointer, see Chapter 2. In C the dereference pointer symbol is * and Rust uses the same symbol.

Thus, if x is a mutable reference or just a reference, then *x is the actual value of variable. The code below shows how we can access the immutable reference:

```
// Pass by immutable reference
fn print_num(x: &i32) {
    println!("{}", *x); // You must dereference to get the value
}

let y = 6;
print_num (&y)
```

Notice that to print out the actual value we use the notation *x, which reads 'dereference x'. We also need to pass the argument in the call as a reference, hence &y. Because the reference is immutable we can't actually change the value of x, only use it in expressions. In many cases this isn't a particularly useful way to pass arguments because the same effect can be had with passing by value and you don't have to dereference the variable.

Of more utility is passing a primitive as a mutable reference.

Mutable Reference: The code below declares a function increment whose job is to increase the integer argument by one. The argument is declared as x: &mut i32, which is a mutable reference.

Inside the function we use dereferencing to manipulate the actual value, thus *x = *x + 1. We could also use the shortcut +=.

In the call to the function we must match the argument using &mut value.

```rust
fn increment(x: &mut i32) {
    *x = *x + 1;  // Dereference and increment, we could also use *x += 1;
}

fn main() {
    let mut value = 10;      // Must be mutable
    increment(&mut value);   // Pass a mutable reference
    println!("Value is now: {}", value);   // Output: 11
}
```

Here is another example with two mutable references, this time using floats:

```rust
fn print_sum (x: &mut f32, y: &mut f32) {
    *x = *x + 5.6;
    *y = *y + 3.4;
    let z = *x + *y;
    println!("The sum is: {}", z);
}

fn main() {
  let mut x = 4.5;
  let mut y = 7.89;
  print_sum(&mut x, &mut y)
}
```

If you're not sure what's going on, I highly recommend you try these examples and observe what happens when you run the code. To summarize here are the four ways to pass a primitive to a function. Take close attention to the **function arguments** and **how we call the function**. Match what you see with Table 16.1 at the end of the chapter.

```rust
// Pass by value
fn print_num1(x: i32) {
    // We don't have to dereference, but you can't change it either
    println!("{}", x);
}

// Pass by value, and mutable inside the function
// Changed value doesn't appear outside the function
```

```
fn print_num2(mut x: i32) {
    x = x + 3;
    println!("{}", x);
}

// Pass by immutable reference
// Not useful in this case, use pass by value instead
fn print_num3(x: &i32) {
    println!("{}", *x); // You must dereference to get the value
}

// Pass by reference, and mutable
fn add_one(x: &mut i32) {
    *x += 1;  // Dereference to gain access to the value
}

fn main () {
  let mut x = 34;
  print_num1 (x); // Notice, no &
  print_num2 (x); // Notice, no &
  print_num3 (&x);  // Notice, no mut
  add_one (&mut x);
  println!("{}", x)
}
```

For non-primitive types the situation is slightly different. The reason is that primitive types are very simple, for example i32 is just four bytes so it's not onerous to copy them.

The common non-primitive types we'll look at are arrays, vectors and strings. They are all handled in a similar way (except perhaps arrays) but we have a section for each one. We'll also look at the compound type struct.

16.4 Passing Arrays To Functions

An array can be passed to a function by value (a copy is made) or by reference (no copy is made).

Pass by Value (Immutable): When passed by value, a **full copy** of the array is made on the function's stack if the array contains one of the primitive types. Otherwise ownership of the contents is passed to the function. For primitive types, this means passing by value ensures that any changes to the array inside the function don't change the array outside the function. To pass by value you just use the name of the array in the function call. You need to careful, however, because if the array is very big there will be a time penalty during the copy. Here is an example of passing an array by value.

```
fn print_array(arr: [i32; 3]) {
    println!("{:?}", arr);
}

fn main() {
    let a = [1, 2, 3];
    print_array(a);
    println!("Original: {:?}", a); // `a` is still usable
}
```

Notice that the array is still accessible after the function returns to the caller.

Pass by Value (Mutable): If you want to change the values of the array inside the function and at the same time pass by value you need to add mut when you declare the argument. Note, the mut in this case doesn't mean the array will change outside the function! The mut is associated with the variable name, not the type. An example is shown below:

```
fn update(mut b:[i32;3]){
    for i in 0..3 {
        b[i] = 0;
    }
    println!("Array inside the function {:?}", b);
    // No need to free the array, its freed when the function exits
}

fn main() {
    let a = [5, 10, 15];
    update(a);

    // The array is still owned by a
    print!("Array after the function has been called {:?}", a);
}
```

Pass by reference (Immutable): If you pass an immutable array by reference, i.e a: &i32, you won't be able to change the array inside the function. If you want to pass by reference and be able to change the array but without changes occurring outside the function, you will need to clone the array inside the function as in, let mut local b = a.clone() and use the clone. However this is the same as passing a mutable array by value which we saw in the above example (Pass by Value (Mutable)). Passing an immutable reference of an array is not so useful in this use case.

Pass by reference (Mutable): If you want the function to be able to change the array that is outside the function then you need to pass the array as a **mutable reference**. Notice that we use &mut in the call as well as the function definition. There is no need to explicitly dereference the array. This is shown in the next code listing.

```rust
fn update(a: &mut [i32;3]){
    for i in 0..3 {
        a[i] = 0;
    }
    println!("Array inside the function  {:?}", a);
}

fn main() {
    let mut a = [5, 10, 15];
    println!("Array before entering the function  {:?}", a);
    update(&mut a);
    print!("Array after the function has been called {:?}", a);
}
```

16.5 Passing Vectors To Functions

Vectors can be passed by value, by reference, or by mutable reference.

Pass by Value: When a vector is passed by value to a function, ownership of the vector is moved to the function. This is not the same as an array where a complete copy is made inside the function. Because the vector changes ownership you can't use the vector after the call returns. Here is an example of this:

```rust
fn consume_vector(v: Vec<i32>) {
    println!("I got a vector with {} elements", v.len());
    // On exit v is dropped, i.e it no longer exists
}

fn main() {
    let my_vec = vec![10, 20, 30];
    consume_vector(my_vec);
    // my_vec can no longer be used here, it's been moved
}
```

If you still want to use call by value and the vector afterwards, you can explicitly return the vector back to the caller, for example:

```rust
fn process_vector(v: Vec<i32>) -> Vec<i32> {
    return v
}
```

```
fn main() {
    let my_vec = vec![1, 2, 3];
    let my_vec = process_vector(my_vec); // ownership returned
    println!("{:?}", my_vec);
}
```

Pass by Reference (Immutable): There is no way to pass by value and not give up ownership unless you return it. Instead call by reference. When calling the function, pass a reference to the vector, that is &my_vec. In the function declaration use v: &Vec<i32>. Note you don't have to dereference the vector as you would do with a primitive type. After the call returns, the original vector is still usable.

```
fn borrow_vector(v: &Vec<i32>) {
    println!("Just borrowing: {:?}", v);
}

fn main() {
    let my_vec = vec![5, 6, 7];
    borrow_vector(&my_vec); // pass by reference
    println!("{:?}", my_vec); // still usable
}
```

Pass by Reference (Mutable): In all these cases we've been unable to change the vector once inside the function. If you want to modify a vector inside a function without taking ownership, you need to pass it as a mutable reference, that is, use &mut Vec<i32>. See the example below:

```
fn add_value(v: &mut Vec<i32>) {
    v.push(42); // modifies the vector
}

fn main() {
    let mut my_vec = vec![1, 2, 3];
    add_value(&mut my_vec); // pass mutable reference
    println!("{:?}", my_vec); // [1, 2, 3, 42]
}
```

16.6   Passing Strings To Functions

There are three ways to pass a string to a function, by value, by reference or by mutable reference.

Pass by Value: As with vectors, if you pass a String to a function by value, you will lose ownership, meaning you won't have access to the string when the function returns. The code for passing a string by value is shown below:

```
fn consume(s: String) {
    println!("Consumed: {}", s);
}

fn main() {
    let name = String::from("Alice");
    consume(name);        // Ownership moved
    // println!("{}", name); // Error: name no longer exists!
}
```

Pass by Reference (Immutable): If you don't need to modify the string, and you still want to use the string after the call returns, pass the string by reference where the string is borrowed by the function. If you don't need to modify the string, this is by far the preferred way to passing a string: it's efficient and the caller doesn't lose ownership of the string. The reference string type is string-slice `&str`.

```
fn greet(name: &str) {
    println!("Hello, {}", name);
}

fn main() {
    let name = String::from("Alice");
    greet(&name);        // &String coerces to &str
    greet("Bob");        // String literal is already &str
    println!({name})     // Ownership is returned and the String is still usable!
}
```

Notice we use `&str` not `&String` in the function call.

Pass by Reference (Mutable): (`&mut String`): Use this when you want to modify the original string inside the function.

```
fn add_world (s: &mut String) {
    s.push_str(' World');
}

fn main() {
    let mut message = String::from("Hello");
    add_world(&mut message);
    println!("{}", message); // Hello World
}
```

16.7   Passing Structs to Functions

As with the compound types, Structs can be passed by value, by reference, or by mutable reference.

Pass by Value: If your struct **only** contains primitive types, then the struct is copied so long as you use the attribute #[derive(Copy, Clone)] (See example). If the struct contain compound types, like strings, vectors etc, ownership of the struct moves to the function and when we exit the function, the struct is destroyed (dropped in Rust language) which means you can't use the data you passed in once the function returns.

```rust
// Ensure struct can be passed by value, only
// works if the fields are primitive types
#[derive(Copy, Clone)]
struct Person {
    height: u32,
    age: u32,
}

fn greet(p: Person) {
    println!("Height = {}", p.height);
}

fn main() {
    let person = Person { height: 10, age: 30 };
    greet(person); // Copy implemented and ownership remains with person
    println!("Height = {}", person.height); // This compiles
}
```

I would, therefore, recommend passing structs by reference unless you are absolutely sure you have no intention of using the struct after the call.

Pass by Reference (Immutable): I recommend using this way to pass a struct to a function, assuming you don't want to change the struct inside the function. Unlike primitive types, **you do not have to dereference** it to use the struct inside the function.

As with the compound types, the function 'borrows' the struct variable in such a way that you get it back when the function returns.

```rust
struct Person {
    name: String,
    age: u32,
}
```

```rust
fn greet(p: &Person) {
    //  No need to dereference p !
    println!("Hello, {}!", p.name);
}

fn main() {
    let person = Person { name: "Alice".to_string(), age: 30 };
    greet(&person); // Borrow, so person can still be used later
    println!("{} is {} years old", person.name, person.age);
}
```

Although this seems redundant since we could do the same with 'pass by value', passing by reference is much more efficient and avoids copying the struct during the call which could be time consuming. Plus if your struct contains compound types, the caller will lose ownership and the struct will be dropped when the function returns.

Pass by Reference (Mutable): Finally, as with arrays and vectors we can use a mutable reference. Not only will you get the data back but you can now also modify it in the function.

```rust
struct Person {
    name: String,
    age: u32,
}

// Notice it's the stuct that mutable not the variable.
fn grow_up(p: &mut Person) {
    //  No need to dereference p !
    p.age += 1;
}

fn main() {
    let mut person = Person { name: "Alice".to_string(), age: 30 };
    grow_up(&mut person);
    println!("{} is now {} years old", person.name, person.age);
}
```

Passing data to functions can seem complex, but with enough practice it will become clearer.

1. If in doubt, passing by reference, (x &type). For a beginner, this should be the preferred approach as it's the least problematic. Not only is it efficient but ownership is retained by the caller.

2. If you need to modify the data inside the function but leave the data outside unchanged you can either clone the data inside the function, or use a mutable pass

by value i.e (`mut x : type`). I would, however, avoid the latter if possible, since copying of compound types is not guaranteed, resulting in loss of ownership by the caller.

3. If you want to modify the data inside and outside the function, use a mutable reference, (`x &mut type`).

When starting out with Rust, I recommend using option one above.

Table 16.1 summarises the calling conventions for the types discussed in this chapter.

Type	Pass Method		Moved?	Mutable?	Notes
`Primitive`	`x:`	`i32`	Copied	No	Original unchanged
	`mut x:`	`i32`	Copied	Yes	Original unchanged
	`x:`	`&i32`	No	No	Read-only reference
	`x:`	`&mut i32`	No	Yes	Mutates original
`Array`	`x:`	`[i32; 3]`	Copied	Yes	Entire array copied
	`x:`	`&[i32; 3]`	No	No	Borrowed array
	`x:`	`&mut [i32; 3]`	No	Yes	Mutable borrowed
`String`	`s:`	`String`	Yes	Yes	Ownership moved
	`s:`	`&String`	No	No	Read-only, is `&str`
	`s:`	`&mut String`	No	Yes	Allows modification
`&str`	`s:`	`&str`	No	No	Common for literals and `String` refs
`Vector`	`v:`	`Vec<i32>`	Yes	Yes	Ownership moved
	`v:`	`&Vec<i32>`	No	No	Read-only reference
	`v:`	`&mut Vec<i32>`	No	Yes	Allows push/pop
`Struct`	`p:`	`Point`	Yes	Yes	Moved unless `Copy`
	`p:`	`&Point`	No	No	Read-only access
	`p:`	`&mut Point`	No	Yes	Fields mutable

Table 16.1: Table of calling methods. Moved refers to ownership being moved. 'Moved unless Copy' in Struct refers to adding the Copy attribute to the struct. Otherwise the stuct is moved and caller loses access to the struct when the function returns.

17

Advanced Topics

The memory management model in Rust is by far the most difficult aspect to learn and understand. If you've come from a programming language such as Python where you hardly ever have to think about managing memory then the Rust approach to memory management will be difficult to comprehend. If you come from a language such as C where memory handling is relatively simple but the programmer is expected to manage memory, you will also have to change the way you think about memory management, but you will be better prepared.

The reason Rust has changed the way memory is managed is to make code written in Rust less likely to have memory related bugs. When writing in programming languages such as C/C++ or Object Pascal, the programmer has to be disciplined to make sure memory is allocated and deallocated properly. It is possible, of course, to write perfectly good code in these languages. In fact the bulk of all code is written this way. The Internet communication protocols, Windows, Linux etc, have all been written this way.

What Rust brings to the table is a compiler that is much more strict in what it lets you do, and in some sense forces a more disciplined approach. This is not to everyone's liking but that is the intent.

Two key concepts in Rust are ownership and borrowing. These two concepts have been mentioned on an off in the previous chapters of the book but let's know look at them in more detail.

17.1 Ownership

In the following code:

```
let x = 5;
```

Rust talks about the variable x as **owning** the number 5. Let's add to this a new line that assigns x to a new variable y:

```
let x = 5;
let y = x;
```

x still owns the value 5, but during the assignment y = x, a **copy** of 5 was made and that copy is **owned** by the new variable y. This will happen to all primitive data types such as integers, Boolean, floating point and characters. Notice that these types have a fixed size that never changes, which makes it easy for the compiler to figure out how to copy them. The minute we deal with things that have variable sizes at runtime, such as strings or vectors, the compiler has no idea what their eventual size might be.

Compared to primitive types, types such as strings or vectors behave slightly differently. For example we might want to create a string:

```
let x = String::from("Hello World");
```

what happens if we add the code y = x?

```
let x = String::from("Hello World");
let y = x
```

Even more interesting, let's try to print the value of x as follows:

```
let x = String::from("Hello World");
let y = x
println!("{}", x);  // Compile error at this line!
```

What might surprise non-Rust programmers is that this code won't compile and you won't be able to run it!

So what's going on? What's happened is that because x owns a non-scalar type, in this case a string, when we call y = x, ownership of the string changes. In the case when x owned a simple integer, the assignment y = x, **made a copy** of the 5 so that x still retained ownership of its own copy of 5. It did this because it was easy and doesn't take much computer time. Because a copy was made, y gets to own its own 5.

However, when we assign the string to y, **no** new copy was made. In fact y sort of steals the string from x and x no longer owns the string. If we try to print the value of x, we'll get a compile error. The compiler doesn't like these kinds of shenanigans and prevents us from running the code. How can we get around this? The easy way is to give y its own copy of the string and leave x still owning the origin copy. The string can be cloned using the `clone()` method:

```
let x = String::from("Hello World");
let y = x.clone();
println!("{} {}", x, y);
```

Output:

```
Hello World
Hello World
```

To summarize:

1. Each value in Rust has a single owner.

2. When you assign a value to another variable, ownership is transferred (this is called a move), unless it's a simple type such as an integer, float, bool or char in which case a copy is made.

3. Rust automatically cleans up the value when its owner is no longer needed, this is sometimes called a drop.

What happens when we call a function with an argument?

If the function is called with a primitive type such as an integer, the function makes a copy of the integer. However, if the argument is a variable such as a string then we have the same issue with ownership as before. Look at the following code:

```
fn call_function (astring: String) {
  println!("{}", astring);
}

fn main() {
  let x = String::from("Hello World");
  call_function (x);
  println!("{}", x); // This line will fail!
}
```

This starts by creating a string x, then passes the string to a function `call_function` which is supposed to print the string. This code will not compile and run! Why not?

When calling the function, ownership of the string passes from x to the function. Once again we have stolen the string from x and x is left without anything. The compiler will warn you of this and prevent you from running the code. What can we do about this? One thing we can try is clone x as we pass it to the function:

```rust
fn main() {
    let x = String::from("Hello World");
    call_function (x.clone());
    println!("{}", x);
}

fn call_function (astring: String) {
    print!("{} ", astring);
}
```

Output:

```
Hello World Hello World
```

This works! By the way, once we leave the function, the cloned copy will disappear.

Although this works, if the string a very long, making a clone would not be very efficient. This is particularly so in the example because all we do with the string is print it out so there is no point in making a copy.

This is where the concept of borrowing comes in.

17.2 Borrowing

The last example showed that in order to pass a string into a function that we wanted to use after the function returns, we had to make a copy using clone() but this is potentially inefficient. What if we could, instead, tell the compiler that the function is merely **borrowing** the string and will give it back afterwards?

If you want to use a value that can be borrowed, you can create a reference. To create a reference we use the ampersand symbol, &, when we pass in the string variable x. Here is an example.

```rust
fn calculate_length(s : &str) -> i32 {
    // len() returns a usize so we cast to covert it to i32
    return s.len() as i32
}
fn main() {
    let x = String::from("Hello World");
    let len = calculate_length(&x);
```

```
    println!("The length of '{}' is {}.", x, len);
}
```

Output:

```
The length of 'Hello World' is 11.
```

First we create the string as before, we then pass a **reference** to the string to our function `calculate_length`. In the function we return the length of the string. The function argument is declared as a reference using `s: &str`, notice the ampersand goes on to the type, not the variable. After we return we can still print out the string, because the function returned ownership to the original owner.

17.3 Mutable References

We'll discuss mutable references in relation to strings. If the function you called needs to modify the string that was passed to it, then we need to change how we declare the function. We still want to create a reference but that reference should be mutable. To do that we use the syntax: `&mut String`. Noticed that when we call the function, we also put `&mut` in front of the variable name, we do this to match the declaration in the function. In the function itself we add a string on to the end of the string we pass in. In essence, we borrow the string, change it, then ownership returns back to the original owner, x.

```
fn change(some_string: &mut String) {
    some_string.push_str(" World");
}

fn main() {
    let mut x = String::from("Hello");
    change(&mut x);
    println!("{}", x); // We've not lost ownereship
}
```

Output:

```
Hello World
```

17.4 Methods

Methods are functions associated directly with a type. An example of a method is the sine trigonometric function. In many languages, to compute the sine of a value we'd type something like `sin (x)`, but in Rust we instead type `x.sin()`. This is an example of a method that is attached to the type of the variable `x`.

We can create our own methods attached to our own types. To do this we define our methods within an `impl` block for the type we want to work with. Here is an example that defines a struct and a couple of methods attached to the struct.

```rust
struct Rectangle {
    width: u32,
    height: u32,
}

impl Rectangle {
    // This is a method
    fn area(&self) -> u32 {
        self.width * self.height
    }

    // This is a static method (also called an "associated function")
    fn new(width: u32, height: u32) -> Rectangle {
        Rectangle { width, height }
    }
}

fn main() {
    let rect = Rectangle::new(10, 5);
    println!("Area: {}", rect.area()); // Using the method
}
```

Notice the use of `self` in the method signatures. This refers to the variable `rect` in the example. The self parameter is special and represents the instance of the type on which the method is being called. It can be borrowed, `&self`, mutably borrowed, `&mut self`, or taken by value, `self`, depending on the method's requirements.

Methods are called using the dot notation unless the method is called `new`, in which case we use the `::` notation. If you're used to object orientated programming you can think of `new` as the constructor.

17.5 Traits

This is an advanced topic so we won't spend too much time on it. But if you've used interfaces (or abstract classes) in languages such Object Pascal, Java, C# and other languages, then the concept of a trait won't be so alien. Traits are effectively interfaces. If you've not come across interfaces then the concept might be hard to grasp initially.

A trait defines a set of methods that types must **implement**, and is similar to interfaces in other languages. This is in contrast to a Rust method which is a function associated with a specific type. A trait can apply to many types, not just one and thus shares functionality.

It's important to appreciate that an interface, that is the trait, is a **contract**, it contains no methods itself. It says, if you implement me, you need to implement all these methods. An interface can be attached to a type and since multiple types can do this, it's a way for different types to share common behavior. For those familiar with object orientated programming, this is a form of polymorphism.

Here is an example of a trait called Shape. Notice it just describes the method signatures, not the implementation!

```
// Define a trait
trait Shape {
    fn area(&self) -> f64;
    fn name(&self) -> &str;
}
```

Let's now define two structs called Circle and Square.

```
struct Circle {
    radius: f64,
}
struct Square {
    side: f64,
}
```

We can now implement the Shape trait for each of these structs. The syntax is impl trait_name for struct_name:

```
// Implement the Shape trait for Circle
impl Shape for Circle {
    fn area(&self) -> f64 {
        std::f64::consts::PI * self.radius * self.radius
    }
```

```
    fn name(&self) -> &str {
        "Circle"
    }
}

// Implement the Shape trait for Square
impl Shape for Square {
    fn area(&self) -> f64 {
        self.side * self.side
    }

    fn name(&self) -> &str {
        "Square"
    }
}
```

Finally, we can create the struct and call the trait methods.

```
fn main() {
    let circle = Circle { radius: 5.0 };
    let square = Square { side: 5.0 };

    println!("{}: {}", circle.name(), circle.area());
    println!("{}: {}", square.name(), square.area());
}
```

Traits can also have associated functions, that is a static method in a trait that is not associated with the type value. They can act like constructors where you might want to initialize a type and return it to the caller. Here is a simple example, where new is an associate function that returns the type via Self. We have also added an argument to new to set the radius of the circle as shown below:

```
// Define a trait with an associated function
trait Shape {
    fn new(r: f64) -> Self;  // associated function: no &self parameter
}

// Implement the trait for a struct
struct Circle {
    radius: f64,
}

impl Shape for Circle {
    fn new(r: f64) -> Self {
        Circle { radius: r }   // default radius
    }
```

```
}

fn main() {
    let c = Circle::new(24.0);   // Call associated function via the type
    println!("Circle radius: {}", c.radius);
}
```

17.6 Dot and Double Colon Syntax

In Rust, the dot syntax (.) and double colon syntax (::) serve different purposes and are used in different contexts:

Dot Syntax: (.)

Used to:

1. Call methods on instances of a type, for example x.cos (3.4)
2. Access fields of a struct, for example, circle.radius
3. Access tuple elements (Not covered in this book)

Here are some real examples that uses the dot notation.

```
struct Person {
    name: String,
    age: u32,
}

impl Person {
    fn greet(&self) {
        println!("Hello, my name is {}", self.name);
    }
}

fn main() {
    let person = Person {
        name: String::from("Alice"),
        age: 30,
    };

    // Accessing a field
    println!("Name: {}", person.name);

    // Calling a method
    person.greet();

    // Accessing tuple elements
```

```
    let point = (10, 20);
    println!("x: {}, y: {}", point.0, point.1);
}
```

Double Colon Syntax: (::)

Used but not limited to:

1. Accessing associated functions (static methods), for example: `let rect = Rectangle::new(10, 5)`
2. Accessing items within namespaces (modules, enums), for example `std::io`
3. Specify paths in the module hierarchy, for example, `my_utils::call_me()`
4. Accessing enum variants, for example, `Direction::North`

Here are some examples of using the double colon:

```rust
struct Rectangle {
    width: u32,
    height: u32,
}

impl Rectangle {
    // Associated function (no &self parameter)
    fn new(width: u32, height: u32) -> Rectangle {
        Rectangle { width, height }
    }
}

enum Color { Red, Green, Blue }

fn main() {
    // Calling an associated function
    let rect = Rectangle::new(10, 5);

    // Accessing enum variants
    let color = Color::Red;

    // Accessing items from standard library
    let v = Vec::<i32>::new();

    // Using a function from a module
    let now = std::time::Instant::now();
}
```

Think of '.' as "do something with this value" and '::' as 'access something from this namespace or type.'

18

Examples

18.1 Factorial

```
// Define a function named 'factorial' that takes a non-negative
// integer as input and returns its factorial
fn factorial(n: u64) -> u64 {
    // Base case: Factorial of 0 is 1
    if n == 0 {
        return 1;
    }

    // Recursive case: Calculate factorial using recursion
    n * factorial(n - 1)
}

fn main() {
    let n = 5; // Define the number for which factorial is to be calculated

    // Call the 'factorial' function with the specified number
    let result = factorial(n as u64);

    // Print the factorial of the number
    println!("Factorial of {} is: {}", n, result);
```

}

Output:

```
Factorial of 5 is: 120
```

18.2 Bubble Sort

```rust
// Bubble sort implementation, sorts vector of integers in ascending order
// Use a mutable reference so that array outside the function is also modified.
fn bubble_sort(array: &mut Vec<i32>) {
    // Outer loop: controls the number of passes through the array
    // After each pass, the largest unsorted element "bubbles up"
    // to its correct position
    for i in 0..array.len() {
        // Inner loop: compares adjacent elements and swap if needed
        // Range shrinks by 'i' at each iteration because the last 'i'
        // elements are already sorted
        for j in 0..array.len() - i - 1 {
            // Compare adjacent values, if left element greater than right, swap
            if array[j + 1] < array[j] {
                // Swap elements to move the larger value toward the end
                array.swap(j, j + 1);
            }
        }
    }
}

fn main() {
    // Create a mutable vector with unsorted integers
    let mut v = vec![2, 2, 10, 1, 5, 4, 3];

    // Sort the vector in-place using bubble sort
    // Pass a mutable reference so the function can modify the original vector
    bubble_sort(&mut v);

    // Print the sorted result: [1, 2, 2, 3, 4, 5, 10]
    println!("{:?}", v);
}
```

Output:

```
[1, 2, 2, 3, 4, 5, 10]
```

www.ingramcontent.com/pod-product-compliance
Lightning Source LLC
Chambersburg PA
CBHW050512210326
41521CD00011B/2424